Easy Spelling's
Sound Dictionary

Unlocking the symphony of language: A vital resource for educationalists, teachers, and parents, revealing the melody of over 4,500 words.

Published by

Heart Space Publications
PO Box 1190
Bakery Hill
Victoria
3350
Australia
Tel +61 450260348
www.heartspacepublications.com
pat@heartspacepublications.com

ISBN: 978-0-6452761-8-3 Print
ISBN: 978-0-6452761-9-0 ePub

Published February 2024 in Melbourne, Australia

Dedication

With gratitude dedicated to Jenny Lamond, whose tireless dedication forms the foundation of this **Sound Dictionary**. Her unwavering commitment and passion have shaped this resource, making it a valuable tool for learners and educators alike.

Acknowledgment

Dr Paul Whiting for his academic guidance in the early part of the **Sound Dictionary** development.

Introduction

Why a Sound Dictionary?

Phonics is like the magic wand that makes spelling less of a mystery and more of an enjoyable puzzle to solve. When students understand the sound of a letter (or letter combination) makes, spelling transforms into a logical sequence of familiar notes. It is akin to learning the melody of a song – once they grasp the sounds as identified by *phonics*, they can confidently string together letters to create words. *Phonics* empowers students to break down words into bite-sized sounds, making it easier to remember how they are spelled. It is the secret weapon that transforms spelling from a daunting task into a fun and engaging journey of decoding and mastering the written word.

The Sounds of English and their Spellings

English words are made from sounds. When written, these sounds are made from letter-combinations, such as the "oo" in book, or "ch" for church. There is a rhythmic dance in the way these combinations, like "ch" or "oo," harmonise to create distinct tones. The beauty lies in their diversity—some, like the gentle "oo" in "book," evoking a soft melody, while others, like the spirited "oo" in "hoop," resonating with a lively cadence. It is a linguistic orchestra where "th" may whisper softly, "ch" may articulate a crisp note, and "sh" may create a subtle hush.

Each sound is represented by a unique letter or letter combinations. This reference manual is meticulously crafted for educationalists, teachers, parents, students, and for those where English is their second or foreign language. It aims to unravel the complexities of English sounds, making it an invaluable tool for enhancing the understanding of language and teaching practices.

The Easy Spelling **Sound Dictionary** is a specialised reference tool for the understanding of pronunciation and phonetic aspects of words in English. Unlike a traditional dictionary that primarily focuses on the meanings and definitions of words, our **Sound Dictionary** places emphasis on the sounds and pronunciation patterns associated with words, using *phonics* instruction. **The Sound Dictionary is a component of the Easy Spelling online spelling and reading course https://EasySpelling.org**.

In our **Sound Dictionary**, these letter combinations play the role of musical notes, allowing learners to decode the language melody. The 42 sounds encapsulate the essence of countless combinations, a testament to the richness and complexity of the English language. They are the building blocks of words, forming a lexical symphony where consonants and vowels, blends and digraphs, dance together, creating a linguistic masterpiece that enriches communication. Just as a skilled musician understands the nuances of each note, our **Sound Dictionary** invites learners to explore the subtleties and variations of these letter combinations, empowering them to navigate the intricate tapestry of English *phonics* with confidence and creativity.

We offer roughly 400 common letter combinations that contribute to the 42 distinct sounds in the Dictionary and referencing over 4,500 sample words. These combinations encompass a diverse array of digraphs, blends, diphthongs, and other phonetic elements that shape the pronunciation and meaning of words. The beauty of this linguistic kaleidoscope lies in its adaptability and the continuous emergence of new combinations, ensuring that English *phonics* remains a vibrant and ever-evolving symphony of sounds. These 42 sounds are combinations of consonants: 4 double consonants: 13 vowel sounds: 7 consonants and vowels and 3 double vowels.

Although this manual is aimed at teachers and parents to teach these *phonics*, the following gives reason why the student would want to be taught these sounds.

Embarking on the journey of language exploration becomes an exciting adventure for students with the introduction of the **Sound Dictionary**. Imagine unlocking the secret code to the world of words, where every pronunciation is a key that opens doors to vibrant stories, creative expression, and confident communication. For students, the **Sound Dictionary** is not just a tool: it is a treasure map leading to the hidden gems of language and spelling mastery, especially if English is a foreign or second language.

In this linguistic quest, students become the heroes of their own narrative, armed with the power to decipher the sounds that weave through the tales of letters and combinations. The **Sound Dictionary** transforms the sometimes perplexing realm of *phonics* into a playground of discovery, where every entry is an invitation to unravel the mysteries of pronunciation, and therefore spelling. Whether diving into the rhythmic cadence of vowel combinations or mastering the crisp notes of consonant blends, students wield the **Sound Dictionary** as their linguistic compass, navigating the twists and turns of the English language with confidence and curiosity.

For students navigating the intricate landscape of English as a second/ foreign language, the **Sound Dictionary** is their compass, guiding them through the rich tapestry of pronunciation and language nuances, helping them unravel English sounds with ease and excitement. It is a key to unlocking the doors of communication and understanding in a new language.

Key features include:

1. **Phonetic Transcriptions:** Accurate representations of the sounds of words using phonetic symbols, providing a visual guide to pronunciation.

2. **Sound Groupings:** Words categorised based on shared sound patterns or phonemes, helping learners recognise and practice similar sounds.

3. **Variations in Pronunciation:** Acknowledgment of regional or dialectical variations in pronunciation, fostering an awareness of diverse linguistic influences.

4. **Authentic Examples and Usage:** Words presented in contextual sentences to illustrate their pronunciation in real-life scenarios.

5. **Global Relevance:** Recognising the growing importance of *phonics* education, many countries have followed the lead of Australia and several U.S. states that have mandated its inclusion in the curriculum. Our manual aligns with these initiatives, catering to the needs of learners worldwide.

6. **Variety of Letter Combinations:** We understand the complexity of English spelling. To address this, we include repeated words, showcasing different letter combinations that contribute to distinct sound groups. This approach enhances the learning experience, allowing users to explore various phonetic patterns.

7. **Time-Saving for Educators:** A valuable resource for teachers, this manual streamlines lesson planning by providing comprehensive content, whilst delivering engaging and effective *phonics* lessons.

8. **Learning a Language other than English:** The Dictionary is a valuable resource for individuals embarking on the journey to learn a second language. Understanding the phonetic nuances and sound patterns early on aids in developing clear pronunciation and effective communication. It offers a foundation for mastering the distinct sounds that form the building blocks of language, and enhancing overall language acquisition. Remember that the International Phonics Alphabet (IPA) is a comprehensive system designed to represent the sounds of any spoken language, so some symbols may represent sounds that are not present in all dialects of English.

9. **Speech Therapists:** While the sophistication of specific tools used by speech therapists may vary, this manual provides a comprehensive and accessible resource for understanding phonetics and sound patterns. It can serve as a supplementary aid in speech therapy sessions, offering clear examples and explanations that support both therapists and their clients. The manual's structured approach to *phonics*, diverse sound categories, and extensive word examples make it a versatile reference for various audiences, including speech therapists working with individuals seeking improvement in articulation, pronunciation, or phonological awareness. While specialised tools may exist for certain therapeutic needs, our **Sound Dictionary** can complement those resources and contribute to a well-rounded approach in language development and speech improvement.

10. **Adaptation to Regional Preferences:** Different countries may require slight adjustments. For instance, Australia, which closely adheres to UK English does have slight differences for the sound groups to that of the UK.

    While we (mainly) default to UK English spelling, we can offer country or cultural preference. **Register with us via pat@heartspacebooks. com if you would like a version with USA English spelling**.

11. **Continuous Improvement:** We encourage feedback from educators, parents, and advanced students. If you suggest enhancements that we implement, we will express our gratitude by sending you a complimentary copy of the upgraded manual.

This manual caters to both academic and non-academic readers, providing valuable insights and accessible content for individuals from various backgrounds and levels of expertise.

Join us in Empowering Learners with Effective *Phonics* **Education!**

Master English Spelling with Easy Spelling

Easy Spelling's Online Spelling and Reading course provides user focused and easy-to-use solutions for mastering English spelling effortlessly.

🔍 Why Choose Easy-Spelling?

- Evidence-based phonic-driven
- Fun and comprehensive for all ages
- From learner to university level
- Engaging spelling and reading games
- Video and audio instructions
- Choose self-text-read or computer-generated 'out-loud' read

🌐 Learn More: Visit http://EasySpelling.org

Dear Purchaser. If you can send proof of purchase of this Sound Dictionary, we will give you a 50% discount for the enrolment (for one student) for our online spelling course. All you need to do is email pat@heartspacepublications.com (with proof of purchase and request the discount).

Contents

A Guide to English Phonics

First, let us clarify some terminology.

Phonics:

- ○ *Definition: Phonics* is a method of teaching reading and spelling that emphasises the relationship between phonemes (the sounds of spoken language) and graphemes (the letters or groups of letters that represent those sounds). It involves teaching individuals to connect the sounds of spoken language with the letters or letter combinations that represent them. Perhaps the easiest way to understand *phonics* is that a "phonic" is simply one unit of sound.

Phonemes:

- ○ *Definition*: Phonemes are the smallest units of sound in a language. They are distinct units of sound that can distinguish one word from another. For example, in English, the words "bat" and "pat" differ only in the initial phoneme (/b/ and /p/).

Graphemes:

- ○ *Definition:* Graphemes are the written representations of phonemes. They can be single letters or combinations of letters that represent a single sound. For instance, in the word "shop," the graphemes are 'sh,' 'o,' and 'p.' Understanding graphemes is crucial for decoding written language.

Navigating the Sound Dictionary:

Jenny's meticulous work has resulted in a user-friendly manual that not only aids memorisation, but also helps students recognise sound patterns within words. Each sound has its own category, with further subdivisions into word families.

For instance, explore the "a" sound in words like "hat," "dance," "trance," and more, reinforcing its diverse applications.

Each word grouping has a sentence of usage to help the student better understand the sound (Maralyn wore her favourite hat to the dance).

Images are often provided as a helpful clue.

Introduction to Blends

Before delving into the **Sound Dictionary**, let us take a moment to explore samples of blends, digraphs, and trigraphs. While these elements are integral to constructing sounds within sound groups, this brief exploration aims to help identify and understand blends, digraphs, and trigraphs more explicitly.

But what is a blend?

Blends, in the realm of *phonics*, are like dynamic duos of consonants that join forces, but maintain their distinct sounds. They occur when two or more consonants appear together in a word, and each contributes its individual sound without blending into a new sound. Blends are the tag teams of *phonics*, allowing us to smoothly combine consonant sounds while preserving their identity. For example, in words like "blow" or "snack," the "bl" and "sn" are blends where the consonants coexist harmoniously, enhancing the phonetic flavour of the word. Understanding blends is a key aspect of *phonics*, as they provide a bridge between individual letter sounds and more complex word structures, making reading and spelling a captivating journey.

Letter Sounds Combinations (Blends and Digraphs)

We commence the focus with simple sounds, such as:
ch in chocolate... say **ch**

sl in slow, where you hear the two separate letters s-l-ow
pl in place
sh in show.
ph (dolphin)
ng (king).

Consonant clusters are groups of consonants that appear together in words, like "scr" in "scrap" or "str" in "street." These clusters can be tricky to spell, but understanding their patterns will help students avoid common spelling mistakes.

Hearing the sounds of the letters is critical in learning to spell. It is also critical in improving reading skills. Students must be able to listen, divide, and identify those sounds.

Below is a short list of the most commonly used letter-combinations. Listen to the sound of each of these as you work through the list.

Letter based combinations

ch	change witch which	bl	blend blind blossom
ck	check crack click	br	brick broke bribe
ng	bang bung bong	cl	clear climb cloak
kn	knight (the k is silent in the 3 words) knife knob	cr	crazy crumbs crate

mb	bomb (the last b is silent) lamb dumb	**dr**	drive drunk dry
ng	standing length single	**fr**	from frame frank
ph	paragraph morph graph	**gl**	gleam glue gloat
sh	show she shame	**gr**	great groan grub
th (voiceless)	think thank throat	**pl**	please police plod
th (voiced)	this they there	**tw**	tweet tweak tweed
wh	which white why	**qu**	quick quack quite
wr	write wrong wreck	**sl**	sleep slow slack
fl	flower flag flew	**sk**	sky ski skill

gr	green grow grill	sc	scrape scope screw
pl	plant play plank	sm	small smile smoke
pr	proud print prank	sp	splattered speak speech
sl	slide slice slumber	st	street stripe stroke
		sw	sweet sweat swat
		tr	travel treat trot

Below are other letter combinations that can confuse. This list has mainly silent letters so see the pronunciations. Such as for the word thumb, where the b is silent;

mn	mb	gh	ice
autumn	dumb (the b is silent in these 4 words)	ghost	concise
hymn	lamb	ghastly	lice

mn	mb	gh	ice
solemn	bomb	laugh	thrice
column	limb	night	excite
damn	womb	thought	
stle	dge	ise	ure
castle	porridge	concise	endure
trestle	fledge	precise	feature
bustle	knowledge	injustice	literature
			manure
ign	ui	tion	ei
design	fruit	station	vein
sign	juice	confection	veil
benign	recruit	operation	reign
align	bruise	citation	eight

Navigating the myriad letter combinations in English may seem like a daunting task, considering there are literally hundreds of them. While committing them all to memory can be challenging, becoming familiar with these combinations proves invaluable. The more accustomed the student is to these patterns, the smoother their spelling endeavours will become.

Understanding how to articulate words with precision can facilitating communication, making it easier for listeners to comprehend what is being said. As an example, some individuals with a foreign accent might pronounce "chocolate" as "shokolate," where the "sh" sound is used instead of "ch." Throughout this manual, pay attention to the pronunciations provided, as they will aid in refining spoken English.

So then, what are digraphs and even trigraphs?

Digraphs and trigraphs are part of the close-knit phonetic families. Unlike blends, which involve consonants combining, digraphs consist of two letters that come together to create a single sound. For instance, in words like "shoe" or "chat," the "sh" and "ch" are digraphs where the letters work in tandem = to produce a distinct sound.

Taking it a step further, trigraphs involve three letters collaborating to produce a unique sound. An example of a trigraph is found in the word "igh" as in "night," where the "igh" works as a single unit to create the sound.

In relation to blends, digraphs, and trigraphs, all these elements contribute to the rich tapestry of *phonics*. While blends showcase the collaboration of consonants without changing their individual sounds, digraphs and trigraphs highlight the synergy of letters working together to produce entirely new phonetic expressions. Together, they form the building blocks of phonetic understanding, making the journey of reading and spelling an intriguing exploration of language.

Here is a short list of trigraphs (three-letter blends).
In this list these are all at the start of a word.

ang	angle bangle fangled
ign	sign (at the end of the word) foreign design
scr	scrap scrape screw
thr	through throat three

gna	gnome gnash gnaw
spr	spray spree sprint

And some more:

str	strand stripe stroll
spl	splint
squ	squad
shr	shred
thr	thrill
scr	scroll
spr	sprite
sch	school
spl	splash
spr	sprout sprint sprinkle
str	strum
scr	script scrape
squ	squat squash squeak
thr	thrive
sch	scheme schlep
spl	splatter splash splendid
scr	scream, scrape script

Above we saw beginning letter-based combinations (**br**ick), what about ending letter-based combinations (be**nd**), or middle letter-based combinations, such as scr**ea**m.

Sample combination vowels sounds: The vowels have different sounds when used together with other letters.

"oo"	sounds like book
"ow"	cow
"or"	horse
"oy"	boy
"ew"	moon
"ear"	beer
"er"	bird
"air"	chair
"ar"	car

Additional examples of combination consonant sounds and their corresponding vowels:

Combination Consonant Sounds:

"ks" – foxes
"gz" – exaggerate
"ks" – mix
"gz" - goggles

Combination Vowel Sounds:

"oo" – cool
"ow" – crown
"or" – north
"oy" – toy
"ew" – few
"ear" – bear
"er" – fern
"air" – fai
"ar" – car

For the teacher or parent teaching the sounds, it goes without saying that the student must be able to accurately reproduce the sounds given, taking notice of the shape of the mouth, tongue, lips, etc.

The Phonics Chart and Explanations

THE INTERNATIONAL PHONETIC ALPHABET (revised to 2015)

CONSONANTS (PULMONIC) © 2015 IPA

	Bilabial	Labiodental	Dental	Alveolar	Postalveolar	Retroflex	Palatal	Velar	Uvular	Pharyngeal	Glottal
Plosive	p b			t d		ʈ ɖ	c ɟ	k ɡ	q ɢ		ʔ
Nasal	m	ɱ		n		ɳ	ɲ	ŋ	ɴ		
Trill	ʙ			r					ʀ		
Tap or Flap		ⱱ		ɾ		ɽ					
Fricative	ɸ β	f v	θ ð	s z	ʃ ʒ	ʂ ʐ	ç ʝ	x ɣ	χ ʁ	ħ ʕ	h ɦ
Lateral fricative				ɬ ɮ							
Approximant		ʋ		ɹ		ɻ	j	ɰ			
Lateral approximant				l		ɭ	ʎ	ʟ			

Symbols to the right in a cell are voiced, to the left are voiceless. Shaded areas denote articulations judged impossible.

CONSONANTS (NON-PULMONIC)

Clicks	Voiced implosives	Ejectives	
ʘ Bilabial	ɓ Bilabial	ʼ	Examples:
ǀ Dental	ɗ Dental/alveolar	pʼ	Bilabial
ǃ (Post)alveolar	ʄ Palatal	tʼ	Dental/alveolar
ǂ Palatoalveolar	ɠ Velar	kʼ	Velar
ǁ Alveolar lateral	ʛ Uvular	sʼ	Alveolar fricative

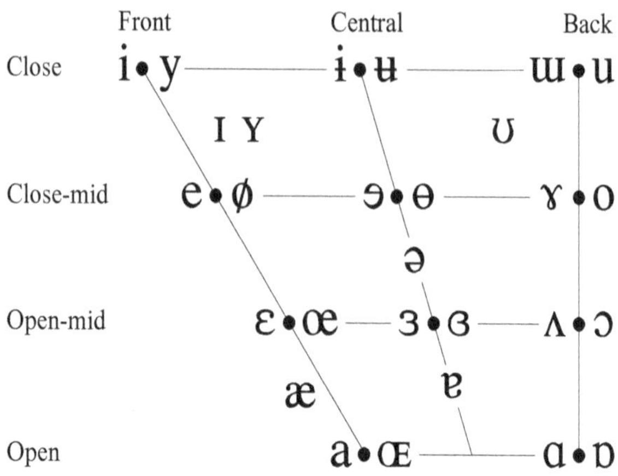

Where symbols appear in pairs, the one
to the right represents a rounded vowel.

DIACRITICS Some diacritics may be placed above a symbol with a descender, e.g. ŋ̊

˳	Voiceless	n̥ d̥	¨	Breathy voiced	b̤ a̤	˷	Dental	t̪ d̪
˅	Voiced	s̬ t̬	˷	Creaky voiced	b̰ a̰	˷	Apical	t̺ d̺
ʰ	Aspirated	tʰ dʰ	˷	Linguolabial	t̼ d̼	˷	Laminal	t̻ d̻
˒	More rounded	ɔ̹	ʷ	Labialized	tʷ dʷ	˜	Nasalized	ẽ
˓	Less rounded	ɔ̜	ʲ	Palatalized	tʲ dʲ	ⁿ	Nasal release	dⁿ
₊	Advanced	u̟	ˠ	Velarized	tˠ dˠ	ˡ	Lateral release	dˡ
₋	Retracted	e̠	ˤ	Pharyngealized	tˤ dˤ	̚	No audible release	d̚
¨	Centralized	ë	˜	Velarized or pharyngealized	ɫ			
ˣ	Mid-centralized	e̽	˔	Raised	e̝ (ɹ̝ = voiced alveolar fricative)			
̩	Syllabic	n̩	˕	Lowered	e̞ (β̞ = voiced bilabial approximant)			
̯	Non-syllabic	e̯	˵	Advanced Tongue Root	e̘			
˞	Rhoticity	ɚ a˞	˵	Retracted Tongue Root	e̙			

OTHER SYMBOLS

ʍ Voiceless labial-velar fricative

w Voiced labial-velar approximant

ɥ Voiced labial-palatal approximant

ʜ Voiceless epiglottal fricative

ʢ Voiced epiglottal fricative

ʡ Epiglottal plosive

ɕ ʑ Alveolo-palatal fricatives

ɺ Voiced alveolar lateral flap

ɧ Simultaneous ʃ and x

Affricates and double articulations
can be represented by two symbols
joined by a tie bar if necessary.

t͡s k͡p

SUPRASEGMENTALS

ˈ Primary stress

ˌ Secondary stress

ˌfoʊnəˈtɪʃən

ː Long   eː

ˑ Half-long   eˑ

˘ Extra-short   ĕ

| Minor (foot) group

‖ Major (intonation) group

. Syllable break   ɹi.ækt

‿ Linking (absence of a break)

TONES AND WORD ACCENTS

LEVEL			CONTOUR		
e̋	or ˥	Extra high	ě	or ˅	Rising
é	˦	High	ê	˄	Falling
ē	˧	Mid	e᷄	˕	High rising
è	˨	Low	e᷅	˔	Low rising
ȅ	˩	Extra low	e᷈	˖	Rising-falling
↓	Downstep		↗	Global rise	
↑	Upstep		↘	Global fall	

Attribution: "IPA Chart, http://www.internationalphoneticassociation.org/content/ipa-chart, available under a Creative Commons Attribution-Sharealike 3.0 Unported License. Copyright © 2015 International Phonetic Association."

Further, the organisation states: The symbol shapes originally devised and approved by the Association may not be preserved in the symbols in any given font. Whether commercial or free, Unicode-compliant or legacy, every font incorporates unique decisions about such elements as line thicknesses, curves, and proportions. In no extant font do all the symbols correspond exactly to the intent of the Association. However, the font mostly used in the 2005 chart, Linguist's Software's IPA Kiel, comes close (* see note below). Therefore a chart made primarily with the IPA Kiel character set best represents the symbols of the IPA. Our use of this font is allowed under our font embedding license.

The 2015 chart makes minor changes to wording and layout, but otherwise reproduces the appearance of the 2005 chart. A few symbol substitutions have been made: The symbol for the labiodental flap, which in the 2005 chart is an extra symbol from Linguist's Software, here comes from the Doulos SIL font (2C71). The symbol for the Close-mid central unrounded vowel is IPA LS Uni 0258; the 2005 chart uses a rotated e. The symbol for the Open-mid central rounded vowel is IPA LS Uni 025E; the 2005 chart uses a rotated closed-omega. The Rising-falling tone letter is IPA LS Uni E9B3, a non-Unicode mapping; the 2005 chart uses a combination of a Minor (foot) group and a circumflex.

Even though most users will not have access to the IPA Kiel font, the Association recommends this version of the chart as an ideal.

* For some time Linguist's Software has offered a "Laser IPA in Unicode" font, IPA LS Uni. This font's symbols are very similar, but not identical, to those of IPA Kiel, and the font is not fully Unicode-compliant.

The International *Phonics* Chart is crucial for anyone learning a language as it provides a visual guide to the sounds of the language. It helps non-academics by offering a systematic way to understand

and pronounce words accurately. By breaking down sounds into categories, like plosives, nasals, fricatives, affricates, liquids, and glides, it simplifies the complexity of language pronunciation. Additionally, the inclusion of combination vowel sounds ensures a comprehensive approach to mastering both individual sounds and their variations. The chart acts as a practical tool for learners, aiding in clearer communication and enhancing language skills, making the learning process more accessible and enjoyable.

The chart, while consisting of symbols, serves as a visual aid to teach school children the relationship between letters and sounds in a language. Here's how it helps:

1. **Sound Representation:** The symbols on the chart represent specific sounds in the language. By associating symbols with sounds, students can better understand how words are pronounced.

2. **Phonemic Awareness:** It fosters phonemic awareness, helping children recognise and manipulate the individual sounds (phonemes) in words. This is a crucial skill for learning to read and spell.

3. **Systematic Learning:** The chart organises sounds into categories (plosives, nasals, fricatives, etc, see below.), providing a systematic approach to learning *phonics*. This helps students grasp the structure and patterns of language sounds.

4. **Pronunciation Guidance:** It offers a reference for correct pronunciation. Students can use the chart to see how different sounds are produced, aiding them in articulating words accurately.

5. **Decoding Skills:** Understanding the relationship between letters and sounds is fundamental for decoding words while reading.

6. **Spelling Assistance:** It aids spelling by illustrating the different ways sounds can be represented by letters. This is particularly useful when introducing spelling rules and patterns.

7. **Visual Memory:** The visual nature of the chart helps in creating a visual memory for the association between symbols and sounds, reinforcing the learning process.

8. **Early Literacy Foundation:** *Phonics* is a key component of early literacy education. The *phonics* chart serves as a foundational tool, helping children build the skills necessary for reading and writing.

In essence, the *phonics* chart is a pedagogical tool that simplifies the complexity of language sounds, making it more accessible for students to learn the building blocks of reading and language.

Seems Complex When first confronted with a /ʃ/ or /æ/ it might seem like a foreign language, at first. The purpose of the IPA in the context of a *phonics* chart is to provide a standardised and precise way to represent speech sounds, not just for English, but all languages. Due to its complexity, the International Phonetic Alphabet (IPA) may initially seem like a foreign language, which is why we advise that students under the age of fifteen may find it challenging. However, for parents who prefer not to delve into the intricacies of the *phonics* chart, our comprehensive and user friendly **Sound Dictionary** (4500 words) provides an excellent alternative. By exploring words within each Sound Group, you can effortlessly enhance your understanding and pronunciation without the need for in-depth knowledge of the IPA.

Throughout the years of spelling instruction using the Jenny Lamond method, the *phonics* chart or symbols were rarely employed. When used, it served as a reference for teachers. However, delving into the explanations is a captivating journey. Once read, it will astonish with the subconscious understanding of how the various sounds are produced.

IPA Chart Explanations

In the chart you will see the following categories:

1. Plosive:

○ **Definition:** Plosives are consonant sounds produced by briefly stopping the airflow and then releasing it with a burst.

Examples: "p" in "pen," "b" in "bag," "t" in "top."
"kuh" – cup
"guh" – gate
"tuh" – tub
"duh" – duck
"puh" – pig
"buh" – bat
"kuh" – key
"guh" – go
"tuh" – tick
"duh" – dip
"cuh" – cat
"buh" – bug
"tuh" – tan
"duh" – dog
"puh" – pod
"buh" – bun

"cuh" – cuff
"guh" – gulp
"kuh" – kite

2. Nasal:

- o **Definition:** Nasals are sounds produced by allowing the air to escape through the nose while blocking the oral passage.

Examples:
"n" in "nest,"
"m" in "mug,"
"ng" in "swing."
"nnn" – nut
"mmm" – map
"nnn" – nap
"mmm" – mitt
"nj" – sing (with a silent g)

3. Trill:

- o **Definition:** Trills are consonant sounds produced by the rapid vibration of one articulator against another. Pronounced with a rapid vibration of the tongue against the alveolar ridge.

Examples: The "r" sound in some Spanish dialects, the "r" in "purr."
"Perro" (dog)

Trill sound in Scottish English:

- o **Word:** "Rural"
- o **Trill Sound:** In some Scottish dialects, the "r" sound is pronounced with a trill.

Trill sound in Italian:

o **Word:** "Ferro" (iron)
o **Trill Sound:** The "rr" in Italian is pronounced with a trill.

Trill sound in Russian:

o **Word:** "Река" (River)
o **Trill Sound:** The "р" (r) in Russian is often pronounced with a trill.

Trill sound in Czech:

o **Word:** "Hrad" (castle)
o **Trill Sound:** The "r" in Czech can be pronounced with a trill.

Trill sound in Portuguese:

o **Word:** "Carro" (car)
o **Trill Sound:** The "rr" in Portuguese is pronounced with a trill.

4. Tap or Flap:

o **Definition:** A tap or flap is a quick, brief movement of one articulator against another.

Examples: The "tt" in "butter,"
The "d" in American English "water."

Tap sound in American English:

o **Word:** "Water"

o **Tap Sound:** The "t" in "water" is pronounced as a quick tap or flap against the alveolar ridge.

o **Word:** "Better"
o **Tap Sound:** The "tt" in "better" is pronounced as a quick tap or flap.

Tap sound in British English:

o **Word:** "Butter"
o **Tap Sound:** The "tt" in "butter" is pronounced with a tap or flap.

Tap sound in Australian English:

- o **Word:** "Kettle"
- o **Tap Sound:** The "tt" in "kettle" is pronounced as a quick tap.

Tap sound in Irish English:

- o **Word:** "Water"
- o **Tap Sound:** The "t" in Irish English is often pronounced with a tap.

5. Lateral Fricative:

- o **Definition:** Lateral fricatives are produced by allowing the airstream to flow over the sides of the tongue.

Uncommon in English, but the Welsh "ll" sound, similar to "th" in "breathe."
"fff" – fan
"vvv" – vine
"thhh" – broth (soft sound)
"th" – think (hard sound)
"sss" – sip
"zzz" – zip
"shh" – ship
"zh" – genre

6. Approximant:

- o **Definition:** Approximants are sounds where the articulators come close to each other but do not create a turbulent airflow.

Examples: "w" in "web," "y" in "yoyo," "l" in "lemon."

7. Lateral Approximant:

- o **Definition:** Lateral approximants involve airflow along the sides of the tongue without creating turbulence.

Examples: "l" in "lemon,"
"l" in "bell."

Here are more English examples of words containing lateral sounds:

Lateral Approximant (/l/):

- o "lamp" (/læmp/)
- o "apple" (/ˈæpəl/)
- o "table" (/ˈteɪbəl/)

Voiceless Lateral Fricative (/ɬ/):

- o Not commonly found in English words, but it is used in some Welsh words like "Llanelli."

Voiced Alveolar Lateral Approximant (/l/):

- o "bell" (/bɛl/)
- o "mellow" (/ˈmɛloʊ/)
- o "will" (/wɪl/)

Voiced Retroflex Lateral Approximant (/ɭ/):

- o Some English dialects may exhibit retroflexion in words like "world" (/wɜrɭd/) or "girl" (/gɜrɭ/).

Voiced Palatal Lateral Approximant (/ʎ/):

- o Not common in English, but it is found in some Spanish loanwords like "tortilla" (/tɔrˈtiʎə/).

English primarily uses the lateral approximant (/l/) in standard Pronunciation, while other lateral sounds are less common or may be influenced by regional accents or loanwords.

These categories help linguists and language learners understand the diverse ways in which speech sounds are produced, contributing to a more nuanced understanding of phonetics.

The terms "consonants (pulmonic)" and "consonants (non-pulmonic)" refer to two categories based on the airflow mechanism involved in producing consonant sounds:

1. Consonants (Pulmonic):

- **Definition:** Pulmonic consonants are sounds produced by using the lungs (the pulmonic airstream mechanism) to generate the airflow. Most consonant sounds in human languages fall into this category.

- **Explanation:** When producing pulmonic consonants, the airflow originates from the lungs. The airstream is then manipulated by the vocal tract and various articulators (such as the tongue, lips, and palate) to create different consonant sounds. Examples include stops (p, b, t, d), fricatives (f, v, s, z), and approximants (w, l, r).

2. Consonants (Non-pulmonic):

- **Definition:** Non-pulmonic consonants are sounds produced without relying solely on airflow from the lungs. Instead, they involve other mechanisms, such as egressive (outward) or ingressive (inward) airflow initiated by other parts of the vocal tract.

- **Explanation:** Non-pulmonic consonants include sounds where the primary airflow is not generated by the lungs. Examples include implosives (sounds created by pulling air inward, e.g., the "clicks" in some African languages) and ejectives (sounds produced by a sudden release of air created by closing the glottis, e.g., the "k" sound in some Native American languages).

In summary, the key difference lies in the source of the airflow. Pulmonic consonants rely on airflow from the lungs, which is the most common mechanism in human languages. Non-pulmonic consonants, on the other hand, involve different mechanisms for initiating or manipulating the airflow, resulting in unique and less common sound types found in specific languages and dialects.

The following categories help linguists describe and classify the diverse range of sounds found in languages based on where the constriction or closure occurs in the vocal tract during articulation. The terms refer to different places of articulation (as per the chart) in the human vocal tract, helping describe where and how sounds are produced. Here is an explanation of each category:

1. **Bilabial:**
   - Articulation: Sounds are produced by bringing both lips together.
   - Examples: "p" in "pen," "b" in "bat."

2. **Labiodental:**
   - Articulation: Sounds are produced by bringing the bottom lip against the upper front teeth.
   - Examples: "f" in "fun," "v" in "van."

3. **Dental:**
   - Articulation: Sounds are produced with the tongue against the upper front teeth.
   - Examples: "th" in "think," "th" in "this."

4. **Alveolar:**
   - Articulation: Sounds are produced with the tongue against the alveolar ridge (the bony ridge just behind the upper front teeth).
   - Examples: "t" in "top," "d" in "dog."

5. **Postalveolar:**
   - Articulation: Sounds are produced with the tongue near or contacting the back of the alveolar ridge.
   - Examples: "sh" in "ship," "zh" in "measure."

6. **Retroflex:**

   - **Articulation:** Sounds are produced with the tongue curled or flexed backward.
   - **Examples:** Uncommon in English, but in some Indian languages, the "t" and "d" sounds are retroflex.

7. **Palatal:**

   - **Articulation:** Sounds are produced with the tongue against the hard palate.
   - **Examples:** "y" in "yellow," "ch" in "chat."

8. **Velar:**

   - **Articulation:** Sounds are produced with the back of the tongue against the soft palate (velum).
   - **Examples:** "k" in "kit," "g" in "go."

9. **Uvular:**

   - **Articulation:** Sounds are produced with the back of the tongue against the uvula.
   - **Examples:** Uncommon in English, but found in some languages like French where the "r" sound is uvular.

10. **Pharyngeal:**

    - **Articulation:** Sounds are produced with constriction in the pharynx.
    - **Examples:** Uncommon in English, but found in some Arabic dialects.

11. **Glottal:**

    - **Articulation:** Sounds are produced with the closure or constriction of the glottis (the space between the vocal cords).
    - **Examples:** "h" in "hat," the glottal stop in the middle of "uh-oh."

Then for the chart let us break down the mentioned categories:

1. **Voiceless Labial-Velar Fricative:**
   - **Description:** This sound is produced by creating friction between the bottom lip and the velum (the back part of the roof of the mouth).
   - **Example:** While not common in English, it can be found in some African languages.

2. **Alveolo-Palatal Fricatives:**
   - **Description:** These sounds are produced with the tongue close to the alveolar ridge and the hard palate simultaneously.
   - **Example:** "sh" in "she," "zh" in "measure."

3. **Voiced Labial-Velar Approximant:**
   - **Description:** This sound involves the approximation of the bottom lip to the velum with voicing.
   - **Example:** Uncommon in English, but found in some indigenous languages.

4. **Voiced Alveolar Lateral Flap:**
   - **Description:** This is a rapid, light contact of the tongue against the alveolar ridge, allowing the air to flow along the sides.
   - **Example:** Uncommon in English but found in some dialects, similar to the "l" sound in "bottle."

5. **Voiced Labial-Palatal Approximant:**
   - **Description:** This sound is produced with voicing and approximation of the bottom lip to the hard palate.
   - **Example:** Uncommon in English, but found in some languages.

6. **Simultaneous and Voiceless Epiglottal Fricative:**
   - **Description:** This sound is produced with the tongue against the epiglottis (cartilage in the throat) without vibration of the vocal cords.
   - **Example:** Uncommon in English but found in some Middle Eastern languages.

7. **Affricates and Double Articulations:**

   - **Description:** Affricates are sounds that begin with an obstruction of the airstream (like a stop) and release into a fricative. Double articulations involve two simultaneous closures in the vocal tract.

   "ch" in "chat" is an affricate.
   "ch" – chew
   "juh" – just
   "ch" – chalk
   "juh" – jungle

8. **Voiced Epiglottal Fricative:**

   - **Description:** This sound is produced with the vibration of the vocal cords and constriction of the epiglottis.
   - **Example:** Found in some dialects of Arabic.

9. **Epiglottal Plosive:**

   - **Description:** This sound is produced by a complete closure of the epiglottis, briefly stopping the airflow.
   - **Example:** Uncommon in English but found in some indigenous languages.

These symbols represent a diverse range of sounds that may not be commonly found in English but exist in various languages around the world. They contribute to the comprehensive representation of the phonetic inventory of different languages.

These terms refer to different tongue positions in the mouth when producing vowel sounds. The terms are often organised based on the height of the tongue (close, close-mid, open-mid, open) and the front-to-back position of the tongue (front, central, back). Additionally, when symbols appear in pairs, the one to the right typically represents a rounded vowel.

1. **Front Vowels:**
   - **Description:** These vowels are produced with the tongue positioned toward the front of the mouth.
   - **Examples:** "ee" in "see," "eh" in "pet."

2. **Central Vowels:**
   - **Description:** These vowels are produced with the tongue positioned in the central part of the mouth.
   - **Examples:** "uh" in "but," "ah" in "father."

3. **Back Vowels:**
   - **Description:** These vowels are produced with the tongue positioned toward the back of the mouth.
   - **Examples:** "oo" in "food," "aw" in "saw."

4. **Close Vowels:**
   - **Description:** These vowels are produced with a relatively small gap between the tongue and the roof of the mouth.
   - **Examples:** "ee" in "see," "oo" in "food."

5. **Close-Mid Vowels:**
   - **Description:** These vowels are produced with a slightly larger gap between the tongue and the roof of the mouth compared to close vowels.
   - **Examples:** "eh" in "pet," "oh" in "go."

6. **Open-Mid Vowels:**
   - **Description:** These vowels are produced with a medium-sized gap between the tongue and the roof of the mouth.
   - **Examples:** "uh" in "but," "aw" in "saw."

7. **Open Vowels:**
   - **Description:** These vowels are produced with a relatively large gap between the tongue and the roof of the mouth.
   - **Examples:** "ah" in "father," "aw" in "saw."

8. **Rounded Vowels:**
   - **Description:** Rounded vowels involve rounding the lips while producing the vowel sound.
   - **Examples:** "oo" in "food" (rounded close back vowel), "aw" in "saw" (rounded open back vowel).

These categories help linguists and language learners understand and categorise the diverse range of vowel sounds found in different languages. The classification is based on tongue position and lip rounding, which are crucial factors in vowel articulation.

Suprasegmentals refer to features of speech that extend over several speech segments, such as stress, pitch, and duration. They are aspects of pronunciation that go beyond individual sounds or segments and influence the entire utterance.

These are:

1. **Primary Stress:**
   - **Description:** It is the most prominent and strongest emphasis placed on a syllable within a word.
   - **Example:** In the word "telegraph," the primary stress is on the second syllable: "te-LE-graph."

2. **Secondary Stress:**
   - **Description:** It is a less prominent emphasis than primary stress and occurs in longer words with multiple syllables.
   - **Example:** In the word "unbelievable," the primary stress is on "lie," and there is secondary stress on "be": "un-be-LIE-vable."

3. **Long:**
   - **Description:** Refers to the duration of a vowel or consonant being extended, typically lasting longer than the corresponding short sound.
   - **Example:** The vowel "ee" in "seat" is long.

4. **Half-Long:**
   - ○ **Description:** An intermediate duration between short and long sounds.
   - ○ **Example:** Found in some languages, like certain varieties of Swedish.

5. **Extra-Short:**
   - ○ **Description:** A very brief duration of a sound, shorter than typical short sounds.
   - ○ **Example:** Found in some languages for certain unstressed syllables.

6. **Minor (Foot) Group:**
   - ○ **Description:** Refers to a grouping of syllables within a word, often connected by rhythm or stress patterns.
   - ○ **Example:** In the word "telephone," the minor foot group might be "TE-le-phone."

7. **Major (Intonation) Group:**
   - ○ **Description:** A larger grouping of syllables within a phrase or sentence, often marked by changes in pitch and intonation.
   - ○ **Example:** In the sentence "I saw a cat and a dog," the major groupings might be "I saw," "a cat," and "a dog."

8. **Syllable Break:**
   - ○ **Description:** The point where one syllable ends, and the next begins.
   - ○ **Example:** In the word "banana," there are three syllable breaks: ba-NA-na.

9. **Linking (Absence of a Break):**
   - ○ **Description:** The absence of a clear break between words or syllables, especially in connected speech.
   - ○ **Example:** In the phrase "cup of tea," the linking creates a smooth transition between "cup" and "of."

These suprasegmentals play a crucial role in the rhythm, melody, and overall prosody of spoken language, contributing to the natural and expressive aspects of communication.

Diacritics are small symbols or marks added to letters or characters in written language to indicate additional phonetic or linguistic information. Diacritics are commonly used in the context of phonetics, phonology, and linguistics to represent specific sounds, stress patterns, or other linguistic features.

Here are some common types of diacritics and their purposes:

1. Phonetic Diacritics:

- These diacritics indicate specific phonetic features or qualities of a sound.
- **Example:** The diacritic for nasalisation (˜) might be added to a vowel symbol to show that the vowel is pronounced with nasal airflow, as in the French word "on."

2. Stress Diacritics:

- Stress diacritics indicate the syllable that receives primary or secondary stress in a word.
- **Example:** The acute accent (´) is often used to mark primary stress, as in the word "résumé."

3. Length Diacritics:

- These diacritics represent the length of a vowel or a consonant.
- **Example:** The colon (:) is used to indicate a long vowel, as in the representation of the long "a" sound in IPA as /a:/.

4. Tone Diacritics:

- Diacritics are employed to represent different tones in tonal languages.
- **Example:** In some African languages, tone marks such as the acute accent or grave accent may be used to distinguish between high and low tones.

5. **Special Pronunciation Diacritics:**
   - Some diacritics are used to indicate specific pronunciation variations or nuances.
   - **Example:** The tilde (~) might be used in the representation of the "th" sound in "this" in some varieties of English.

6. **Historical or Etymological Diacritics:**
   - Diacritics may be used to preserve historical or etymological information about a word.
   - **Example:** The diaeresis (¨) might be used to indicate that two adjacent vowels are pronounced separately, as in "coöperate."

7. **Miscellaneous Diacritics:**
   - There are various other diacritics used for specific linguistic purposes, such as the macron (¯) to indicate vowel length or the cedilla (¸) to modify the pronunciation of a "c" or "s."

Diacritics play a crucial role in linguistic analysis and precise transcription, providing a way to represent fine distinctions in pronunciation or linguistic features that might not be apparent from the basic letters of an alphabet. They are often used in systems like the International Phonetic Alphabet (IPA) to represent sounds in a standardised and detailed manner.

These terms refer to various diacritics used in phonetics to specify additional features or qualities of speech sounds. Here is an explanation for each of them:

1. **Voiceless:**
   - **Description:** Indicates that a sound is produced without vibrating the vocal cords.
   - **Example:** Voiceless plosives like "p," "t," and "k."

2. **Breathy Voiced:**
   - **Description:** Indicates that a sound is produced with simultaneous vocal cord vibration and a slight opening, allowing some breathiness.

- o **Example:** The "h" sound in Hindi, where breathy voicing can be heard.

3. **Dental:**
   - o **Description:** Indicates that a sound is produced with the tongue against the upper front teeth.
   - o **Example:** The "th" sounds in "think" and "this."

4. **Voiced:**
   - o **Description:** Indicates that a sound is produced with vocal cord vibration.
   - o **Example:** Voiced sounds include most vowels and consonants in English.

5. **Creaky Voiced:**
   - o **Description:** Indicates that a sound is produced with a low and creaky vocal cord vibration.
   - o **Example:** Found in some speech patterns or dialects.

6. **Apical:**
   - o **Description:** Indicates that a sound is produced with the tip of the tongue.
   - o **Example:** The "t" and "d" sounds in some dialects where the tongue tip touches the alveolar ridge.

7. **Aspirated:**
   - o **Description:** Indicates a burst of air accompanying the release of a plosive.
   - o **Example:** The initial sounds in "pat" and "bat."

8. **Linguolabial:**
   - o **Description:** Indicates that a sound is produced with the tongue against the upper lip.
   - o **Example:** Uncommon in English but found in some African languages.

9. **Laminal:**
   - **Description:** Indicates that a sound is produced with the blade of the tongue.
   - **Example:** Laminal fricatives like the "sh" sound.

10. **More Rounded:**
    - **Description:** Indicates that the lips are rounded to a greater degree.
    - **Example:** The "oo" sound in "food."

11. **Labialised:**
    - **Description:** Indicates that a sound is produced with rounding of the lips.
    - **Example:** The "w" sound in "web."

12. **Nasalised:**
    - **Description:** Indicates that a sound is produced with nasal airflow.
    - **Example:** The nasalised vowels in French, like in "on" and "an."

13. **Less Rounded:**
    - **Description:** Indicates that the lips are rounded to a lesser degree.
    - **Example:** The "ee" sound in "see."

14. **Palatalised:**
    - **Description:** Indicates that a sound is produced with the tongue approaching the hard palate.
    - **Example:** The "sh" sound in "ship."

15. **Nasal Release:**
    - **Description:** Indicates that air is released through the nose during the release of a plosive.
    - **Example:** Common in some African languages.

16. **Advanced:**
    - **Description:** Indicates that a sound is produced with the tongue moved forward.
    - **Example:** The "ee" sound in "see."

17. Velarised:

- o **Description:** Indicates that a sound is produced with the back of the tongue approaching the velum.
- o **Example:** The "ng" sound in "sing."

18. Lateral Release:

- o **Description:** Indicates that air is released along the sides of the tongue.
- o **Example:** Common in some English dialects, like the "t" sound in "bottle."

19. Retracted:

- o **Description:** Indicates that a sound is produced with the tongue moved backward.
- o **Example:** The "aw" sound in "saw."

20. Pharyngealised:

- o **Description:** Indicates that a sound is produced with constriction in the pharynx.
- o **Example:** Found in some Arabic dialects.

21. No Audible Release:

- o **Description:** Indicates that there is no audible burst of air during the release of a plosive.
- o **Example:** Common in some dialects.

22. Centralised:

- o **Description:** Indicates that a sound is produced with the tongue moved toward the center of the mouth.
- o **Example:** The "uh" sound in "but."

23. Mid-Centralised:

- o **Description:** Indicates that a sound is produced with the tongue positioned somewhat in the center.
- o **Example:** Found in some vowel variations.

24. Raised (= Voiced Alveolar Fricative):

- o **Description:** Indicates that a sound is pronounced with the tongue raised, often representing a specific fricative sound.
- o **Example:** The "th" sound in "this."

25. Syllabic:

- o **Description:** Indicates that a consonant can function as the center of a syllable.
- o **Example:** The "l" sound in the final syllable of "bottle."

26. Lowered (= Voiced Bilabial Approximant):

- o **Description:** Indicates that a sound is pronounced with the tongue lowered, often representing a specific approximant sound.
- o **Example:** The "w" sound in "web."

27. Non-Syllabic:

- o **Description:** Indicates that a vowel is pronounced as part of a consonant, not forming a separate syllable.
- o **Example:** The "i" in the final syllable of "nation."

28. Advanced Tongue Root:

- o **Description:** Indicates that the root of the tongue is moved forward.
- o **Example:** Found in some African languages.

29. Rhoticity:

- o **Description:** Indicates the presence of the rhotic "r" sound.
- o **Example:** The "r" sound in some English dialects.

30. Retracted Tongue Root:

- o **Description:** Indicates that the root of the tongue is moved backward.
- o **Example:** Found in some African languages.

These diacritics are crucial for phonetic transcription and analysis, allowing linguists to capture subtle variations in speech sounds and pronunciation across different languages and dialects.

Here is how it can help a student:

1. **Consistency:** The regular alphabet does not always represent sounds consistently. For example, the letter 'a' can have different sounds in words like "cat" and "car." The IPA provides a consistent symbol for each specific sound, eliminating ambiguity.

2. **Clarity:** It helps learners distinguish between similar sounds that might be represented by the same letter. For example, the sounds in "ship" and "sheep" are different, and the IPA symbols /ʃ/ and /iː/ make this distinction clear.

3. **International Understanding:** The IPA is an international standard, so learners and teachers worldwide can communicate about sounds without being hindered by language barriers.

4. **Pronunciation Guide:** For learners of a second language, the *phonics* chart with IPA symbols can serve as a guide for correct pronunciation. They can look at the symbol and associate it with the specific sound, aiding in accurate pronunciation.

5. **Sound Analysis:** The chart allows learners to break down words into individual sounds. For example, the word "ship" can be analysed as /ʃɪp/, helping learners understand the components of the word.

While it may take a bit of practice to become familiar with the IPA symbols, it becomes a valuable tool for those who are serious about understanding and mastering the phonetics of a language. It is particularly helpful for language learners, linguists, and educators aiming for precision in describing and teaching speech sounds.

The IPA symbols themselves might not be immediately intuitive to someone unfamiliar with them. The key to understanding them lies in learning the associations between the symbols and the actual sounds they represent. Here are some examples:

1. **/ʃ/ - The "sh" Sound:** The symbol /ʃ/ represents the "sh" sound, as in "ship." While the symbol may not look like the letters "sh," it is a standardised representation used by linguists and educators. When learning, a student would be taught that this symbol corresponds to the "sh" sound.

2. **/ɪ/ - The "ih" Sound:** The symbol /ɪ/ represents the short "ih" sound, as in "ship." Similarly, students need to be taught that this symbol corresponds to the specific vowel sound in "ship."

So, when you see /ʃɪp/, you break it down into two parts: /ʃ/ (sh sound) and /ɪ/ (ih sound). It is through this breakdown that you can understand how to pronounce the word "ship."

In a learning context:

- The teacher would introduce the symbol /ʃ/ and associate it with the "sh" sound.

- The teacher would also introduce /ɪ/ and associate it with the short "ih" sound.

- By combining these symbols, the student learns to associate /ʃɪp/ with the correct pronunciation of "ship."

It is indeed a process that involves instruction and practice, and the goal is for the symbols to become familiar over time.

Below is a list of some common IPA chart symbols along with the English sounds they represent. Note that this is not an exhaustive list, as there are many more symbols in the IPA Chart representing various sounds, including those from different languages. Additionally, English spelling can be irregular, so the relationship between letters and sounds is not always straightforward.

Consonants:
- /p/ - voiceless bilabial plosive (as in "pen")
- /b/ - voiced bilabial plosive (as in "bat")
- /t/ - voiceless alveolar plosive (as in "top")

- /d/ - voiced alveolar plosive (as in "dog")
- /k/ - voiceless velar plosive (as in "cat")
- /g/ - voiced velar plosive (as in "go")
- /f/ - voiceless labiodental fricative (as in "fan")
- /v/ - voiced labiodental fricative (as in "van")
- /θ/ - voiceless dental fricative (as in "think")
- /ð/ - voiced dental fricative (as in "this")
- /s/ - voiceless alveolar fricative (as in "snake")
- /z/ - voiced alveolar fricative (as in "zebra")
- /ʃ/ - voiceless postalveolar fricative (as in "shoe")
- /ʒ/ - voiced postalveolar fricative (as in "genre")
- /h/ - voiceless glottal fricative (as in "hat")
- /m/ - voiced bilabial nasal (as in "mat")
- /n/ - voiced alveolar nasal (as in "net")
- /ŋ/ - voiced velar nasal (as in "sing")
- /l/ - voiced alveolar lateral approximant (as in "lip")
- /r/ - voiced alveolar tap or flap (as in "red")
- /j/ - voiced palatal approximant or glide (as in "yes")
- /w/ - voiced labiovelar approximant or glide (as in "win")
- /p̪/ - voiceless labiodental plosive (as in "pat")
- /b̪/ - voiced labiodental plosive (as in "bat")
- /t̪/ - voiceless dental plosive (as in "tot")
- /d̪/ - voiced dental plosive (as in "dot")
- /t͡ʃ/ - voiceless postalveolar affricate (as in "chat")
- /d͡ʒ/ - voiced postalveolar affricate (as in "judge")
- /ʔ/ - glottal stop (as in "uh-oh")
- /m̥/ - voiceless bilabial nasal (as in some pronunciations of "hymn")
- /n̥/ - voiceless alveolar nasal (as in some pronunciations of "ink")
- /ŋ̥/ - voiceless velar nasal (as in some pronunciations of "sink")

Vowels:

- /i/ - close front unrounded (as in "see")
- /ɪ/ - near-close near-front unrounded (as in "sit")
- /e/ - close-mid front unrounded (as in "bet")
- /ɛ/ - open-mid front unrounded (as in "pet")
- /æ/ - near-open front unrounded (as in "cat")

- /ɑ/ - open back unrounded (as in "father")
- /ɒ/ - open back rounded (as in "lot")
- /ʌ/ - open-mid back unrounded (as in "cup")
- /ʊ/ - near-close near-back rounded (as in "book")
- /u/ - close back rounded (as in "boot")
- /o/ - close-mid back rounded (as in "boat")
- /ɪə/ - diphthong (as in "near")
- /eə/ - diphthong (as in "air")
- /ʊə/ - diphthong (as in "tour")
- /aɪə/ - triphthong (as in "fire")
- /aʊə/ - triphthong (as in "hour")

Diphthongs:

- /eɪ/ - diphthong (as in "day")
- /aɪ/ - diphthong (as in "light")
- /ɔɪ/ - diphthong (as in "coin")
- /aʊ/ - diphthong (as in "house")

These symbols represent a variety of English sounds, and mastering them involves associating each symbol with its corresponding sound. Phonetic transcriptions use these symbols to accurately represent the pronunciation of words.

A Schwa vowel

The schwa is a vowel sound that is often described as a mid-central, unstressed, and relaxed (some call it lazy) vowel. In the International Phonetic Alphabet (IPA) chart, it is represented by the symbol [ə]. The schwa sound is typically found in unstressed syllables and is pronounced as a short, neutral, or "uh" sound. It is the most common vowel sound in English.

Examples of the schwa sound in English:

- "sofa" (sə-fa)
- "banana" (bə-næ-nə)

In terms of consonants, there is not a specific consonant sound referred to as a "schwa consonant." However, the schwa sound can sometimes influence the way certain consonants are pronounced, especially when they occur in unstressed syllables. For example, in some cases, consonants like /l/, /n/, and /r/ can be pronounced with a schwa-like quality when they appear in unstressed syllables. This phenomenon is known as "syllabic consonants," where the consonant takes on a more vowel-like role. This is especially noticeable in words like "bottle" (/bɒtəl/) or "button" (/bʌtən/), where the final syllable contains a syllabic consonant with a schwa-like quality.

An unspoken sound, on the other hand, typically refers to a complete absence of audible speech sound. For instance, when we encounter silent letters in words, those letters do not represent sounds when the word is spoken. In contrast, the schwa sound is a vowel that is indeed pronounced, but it is often subtle and less prominent than stressed vowels. Unspoken sounds are typically associated with silent letters in words. Here are five examples of words with unspoken sounds:

Debt: the "b" in "debt" is silent. The word is pronounced "det."
Knight: the "k" in "knight" is silent. The word is pronounced "nyt."
Honest: the "h" in "honest" is silent. The word is pronounced "on-est."
Calm: the "l" in "calm" is silent. The word is pronounced "kam."
Resign: the "g" in "resign" is silent. The word is pronounced "ri-zain."

In each of these examples, one or more letters are not pronounced when speaking the word. These silent letters do not contribute to the spoken sound of the word but may have historical or etymological reasons for being present in the spelling.

The plosives:

Here are eight more words for sounds where the air flows past the tongue (liquids) and glides:

Liquids:
"lll" – bell
"lll" – olive
"lll" – balloon

Glides:
"rrr" – rip
"wuh" – wet
"yuh" – yellow
"huh" – hill
"wuh" – wand

The Six Stages of Phonics Instruction

Trying to commit the entire **Sound Dictionary** to memory might be ambitious, but familiarising the student with the forty-two sounds proves invaluable. This familiarity facilitates the recognition of sound patterns, enhancing spelling skills. But let us start at the beginning.

It is crucial to present sounds in manageable portions during *phonics* instruction, as overwhelming students can lead to confusion. Allow students to construct their understanding in a controlled and well-paced manner, considering their attention span.

As a teacher or parent, it is essential to recognise the student's attention span and avoid exceeding it. While there are six generally identified steps, it is important to tailor these based on the student's age and prior exposure to *phonics*.

Step One – Awareness

In this initial stage, students learn to recognise common sounds associated with the alphabet, such as "a" for apple and "b" for book. Introduce a few two or three-letter words where the sounds are emphasised.

Step Two – Growing Awareness

Continue reinforcing the sounds of the alphabet and introduce more two or three-letter words. At this point, there is no focus on vowels or consonant-to-vowel combinations.

Step Three – Digraphs, Short and Long Sounds

As students develop an understanding of alphabet sounds, shift the focus to teaching when each letter says either:

Its sound (short sound), as in "c" for cat,
Or says its name (long sound), as in "a" for apron.

Introduce longer words and start to identify vowels.

Step Four – Continue with Digraphs and Trigraphs

Emphasise familiarity by introducing slightly longer words with two or three syllables. Encourage students to recognise sounds within each syllable and identify vowels.

Step Five – Confidence

Continue exploring vowel and consonant combinations, including more trigraphs, blends, and multiple-syllable words.

Step Six – Mastery

Expand the knowledge base to include all forty-two sound groups, encompassing digraphs, trigraphs, and blends (as per the **Sound Dictionary** below).

This stage integrates spelling rules. As the teacher assesses the student's progress and adjust the pace of each stage accordingly, modifying the duration of sessions as needed.

Although there are six recognised steps, the number of learning periods will in all probability be many more than six. Some steps will require more learning periods than others. To start with the tutor will have a 100% hands-on support. But as the steps are advanced there will be more "student only" work.

Other Suggestions

It is helpful to look for small words in larger words

Such as, friend has an **end** in it, and benefit has **ben** and **fit** fitting together.

Here's a short list of words with smaller words within them:

- Friend - end
- Doctor - (be sick **or** go to the doctor)
- Listen - (I've told you **ten** times to listen)
- Monster - (you go **on** about the monster)
- Problem - (as a **pro** speller you have no problem)
- Universe - (sing a nice **verse** about the universe)
- Adventure - vent
- Butter - but, utter
- Garden - (a garden is your outside **den**)
- Elephant - (the **ant** came at the end of the elephant)
- Writer - write
- Calendar - end, lend
- Master - mast
- Example - (in the example you have **ample exam** time)
- Computer - (you put **put** in a computer)
- Telescope - (you **scope** the telescope)
- Chocolate - (don't be **late** for chocolate)
- Christmas - Christ
- Holiday - day
- Bicycle - (you **cycle** on your bicycle)
- Breakfast - break, fast (compound word)
- Sandwich - sand, which
- Camera - (it was an **era** when the camera **came**)

- Bedroom - bed, room (compound word)
- Airport - air, port
- Rainbow - rain, bow
- Keyboard - key, board
- Sunshine - sun, shine (the **sun shine**d)
- Laughter - laugh
- Eleven - even
- Balance - lance
- Suddenly - sudden, den
- Remember - member
- Happening - happen
- Elevator - elevate, or
- Birthday - birth, day
- Morning - morn
- Furniture – you have fur and a nit in your furniture
- Jumping - jump
- Examine - exam
- Organise - organ
- Artificial - art, official
- Confuse - con, fuse
- Airport - air, port
- Grandmother - grand, mother

These examples continue the pattern of breaking down words into smaller components.

Mnemonics

Mnemonics are memory aids that assist students in recalling information more effectively. Here is a sentence demonstrating how to use mnemonics:

"To remember the order of the planets from the sun, use the mnemonic 'My Very Educated Mother Just Served Us Noodles,' where each word's first letter corresponds to a planet (Mercury, Venus, Earth, Mars, Jupiter, Saturn, Uranus, Neptune)."

Explore the following mnemonics examples designed to assist in remembering the correct spellings of various words.

a (angel) Sayings its name (long)

A mouse did prance in a trance. To finance a mousey dance. Lost its balance, what a glance! Called the mouse ambulance.

In attendance, a wise old owl, With a hoot and a scowl, Said, "Consider circumstance, Learn the importance of mousey extravagance!"

Why did the ant attend the pageant?
Because it wanted to be plant-tastic and show off its slant-y dance moves, but it forgot its pants, so it had to pant through the entire chant!

a (dance) Saying its sound (short)

At the **entrance** of the **dance**, Joe seized a **glance**, captivated by the **performance** of Mary, lost in a spellbinding **trance**. As the music **enchants**, romance...

Within the **Sound Dictionary** below there are around 250 sentence mnemonics.

Jenny's Sound Dictionary

As you embark on this journey, you are set to explore words within the forty-two sound groups. The introductory word in each list is underlined for clarity. Take the word "dance," for instance, where the letters "ance" are highlighted. Now, scan the other words in that group for the recurring "ance" pattern. Move on to the next line, where "ant" is underlined, signalling the starting point for that group. Consistency in patterns becomes evident as you explore the table.

This table meticulously organises the forty-two sounds based on their relevance in spelling mastery. While it may not be exhaustive, it encompasses enough to provide you with a robust understanding of these sounds.

For young students we recommend tackling only two or three smaller groups in one session or focusing on one larger group. Older or more advances students can take on more sounds. This deliberate approach enhances retention. It is advisable to revisit the Sound Groups at least three times to reinforce understanding effectively.

The Sound Dictionary = a dictionary per sound type.

Used for any word where the student can not **talk to the pencil** (sounding out aloud) for words they do not recognise, it is a safety net. They will get to know the spelling of a word as you place it with words they already know. For instance, with the letter combination **ough** (thr**ough**, t**ough**) that Jenny calls *'oh u go home'* words. It is about finding letter combinations (of which you will soon see are many {some 400}) and becoming familiar with the combinations.

Another combination is **au**ntie uncle words, where there is the letter combination of **au** (which may have a **/or/** sound in the word). Examples of these are **au**ditorium, or **Au**stralia. L**au**ndry is another. Within this **Sound Dictionary** there are many such letter combinations, where words that have those letter combinations are grouped.

As a way to remember some of these **au**ntie uncle words, you can use the many stories or poems that Jenny thoughtfully created these mnemonics for us, such as; The Australian restaurant behind the auditorium has a laundry. Better still, get the student to create his or her own.

Four hundred sound combinations

This table organises sounds based on their effectiveness in teaching remedial reading and spelling. It is important to note that the table does not include a specific category for the indefinite sound. Instead, the various spellings of this sound are classified under the nearest represented sound, emphasising the importance of clear and precise speech.

apple	angel	elephant	emu	igloo	ice	dog	open	umbrella	uniform	look	moon	cow	boy
a	a	e	e	i	i	o	o	u	u	oo	oo	ow	oy
ai	a-e	ea	e-e	y	i-e	a	o-e	o	u-e	oul	o	ou	oi
	ai	ie	ee	u	ie	au	oa	ou	ue	u	wo	hou	uoy
	ea	ai	ey	o	y	oh	ow	oe	eau	o	oe	ough	
	ay	u	ea	ie	igh	ho	ough	oo	ew		oeu		
	et	a	is	e	eigh	ou	owe	up	ewe		ou		
	ey	ay	i	ui	eye	ow	oh	a	eu		u		
	ei	ei	eo	hi	ye	eo	oe		iew		ue		
	eig	ae	ie	he	is		ou		ieu		ui		
	ae	eo	ay	ei	ais		ew		eue		ew		
	eigh		ei		ei		eau		ui		eu		
	aigh		y		uy		au		you		ough		
	ao		oe				oat		yew				
	au		ae				oo						
							ot						
							eo						

run	car	her	air	deer	or	kit	seal	gulf	jug	lip	fox	van	th	she
r	ar	er	air	eer	or	k	s	g	j	l	f	v	th	sh
rr	are	err	are	ear	ort	ke	se	gu	g(e)	ll	ff	ve	the	shi
wr	au	ear	ear	ere	ore	kk	ss	gue	g(i)	lle	fe	f		s
rh	ah	re	eir	er	oar	lk	ps	gg	g(y)	le	ffe	lve		ss
	a	ere	heir	ir	(hor)	kh	st	gh	gg	el	lf	ph		ssi
	arre	ir	ar	ier	our	que	sw		dge	al	ph			si
	arrh	ar	aire	eir	oor	qu	sth		dg	il	pph			xi
	aar	yr	ere		ough	g	c(e)		dj	ol	gh			ti
	ear	yrrh	aer		aw	c	c(i)		di		u			ci
	er	or	ayer		awe	cc	c(y)				ft			sc
	at	our	ayor		au	ch	sc							sci
		olo			hau	ck								ce
		ure			aur	cch								ch
		ur			ar	cq								cho
		urr			al	cqu								
					augh									
					ure									

chip	tap	zoo	box	yet	win	man	not	bang	dog	bin	pin	hat	measure
ch	t	z	x	y	w	m	n	(i)ng	d	b	p	h	s
tch	te	ze	xe	i	u	mm	nn	(a)ng	de	bb	pp	wh	si
ti	tt	ss		j	wh	me	ne	(o)ng	dd				
c	tte	zz		u	o	gm	en	(u)ng					
	dt	s				mb	in	(e)ng	d				
	ct	se				mn	on	ngue					
	cht	x				om	ain	n					
	pt	's				lm	eign						
	bt					mme	kn						
	th						dne						
	ed						nd						
							pn						
							gn						
							mn						
							gne						
							an						

So, here we go…

a (apple)				Sound Group 1
apple				
hat				
dance trance prance glance	entrance distance balance finance hindrance	importance appearance attendance ambulance reliance	extravagance significance acquaintance circumstance performance	a
At the entrance of the dance, Joe seized a glance, captivated by the performance of Mary, lost in a spellbinding trance. As the music enchants, romance…				
ant chant pant grant plant slant	migrant remnant constant pageant vacant	ignorant tolerant observant defiant reluctant	insignificant superabundant communicant luxuriant participant	
In the enchanting forest, joined the chant of a mystical pant, where nature's spirit granted life to every plant.				
plait plaid				ai

💡 **The sound /ae/ presents little difficulty. Words ending in – ant and – ance are a problem, so collecting them here using ant and dance for clues is helpful. See also Sound Group 37 (an). In normal speech, of course, the sound of the a in many of these words is indefinite (schwa) /ə/.**

a (angel) Sayings its name (long sound)				Sound Group 2
angel apron dais	apricot donator curator	escalator incubator incinerator		a
How did the angel get to the top of the apricot tree. She caught the escalator				
sundae	Why did the plate break up with the sundae? It couldn't handle the rocky road to dessert and needed some "bowl-ing" time to find a better match!			ae
gate plate grape chase pane frame create	inhale mistake membrane dictate rename	separate propagate centigrade stimulate hurricane	congratulate supermundane appropriate substantiate calculate	a-e
It's inappropriate to inhale so deeply because you create a hurricane when you exhale.				
play bay clay sway spray	display repay array astray dismay		yesterday Saturday overlay stowaway	ay
Yesterday, Saturday the stowaway to his dismay could not pay and so went astray at the bay.				
train paid stain aim fail bait	remain restrain afraid mermaid disdain	preordain porcelain chamberlain ascertain entertain		ai

The mermaid failed to catch the train because she was afraid.				
trait				ait
straight				aigh
gaol				ao
gauge (if needed, put in your **Decoding Book** with other rare irregular words.)				au
grey prey they whey	they	obey convey survey	abeyance Reynard	ey
In the meadow, a grey hare obeys nature to stalks its prey. Reynard surveys what they are up to.				
reins vein veil	skein	surveillance reindeer	heinous	ei
reign	feign	design		eig
eight freight weight (y) weigh sleigh neigh	eighty eighteen neighbour	outweigh	Our eight neighbours - My weight, eight kg's - My height, eight feet.	eigh
break steak great				ea
Great – time for a steak break.				
ballet valet beret chet	bouquet parquet crochet croquet	ricochet tourniquet		et
At the ballet, the valet, wearing a blue beret carried the bouquet of flowers.				
fete				e

e (egg) Sayings its sound (short sound)					Sound Group 3
hen fed well hem step beg	velvet legend tempest helmet elect	excellent effervesce cemented tenement semester	embezzlement benevolent embellishment enlightenment-		e
The helmet wearing hen caused a tempest after someone fed on her excellent eggs.					
bread meant breadth spread tread	wealthy feather treasure heaven threading	endeavour pleasantry treachery measurement threatening	leatheriness		ea
You **eat** your br**ea**d and spr**ea**d on your br**ea**d					

I spread myself out with my head on the heather.

This was to give me a measure of pleasure.

The sky was like lead, and threatened bad weather.

I dreamt about death and heaven and treasure.

I knew that endeavour with thread and good leather would give me great wealth and surely some treasure.

That bread, baked with leaven as light as a feather would give me good health and certainly pleasure.

A peasant was I and as deaf as could be, but I read heavy books, for my eyes could see. I had no dread of ill for my breath was steady, I leapt towards great wealth with no stealth in my tread.

I hoped for good health, and meant to find wealth, but instead I found wealth right there in good health.

heifer	their	leisure	leisurely	leisureliness	ei
friend					ie
said					ai
says					ay
many	any	anyone	anything		a
bury					u
leopard					eo
aeroplane aerobatics aerodynamics haemorrhage					ae
Which one word does not fit with the others?					

<table>
<tr><td colspan="5">e (me) Sayings its name (long short)</td><td>Sound Group 4</td></tr>
<tr>
<td>me
he
we
de...
pre...
re...</td>
<td>sesame
simile
acme
anemone
create</td>
<td>museum
hideous
courteous
plenteous
stereo (type)</td>
<td></td>
<td></td>
<td>e</td>
</tr>
</table>

Me + he (we) ate sesame.

<table>
<tr>
<td>trapeze
cede
swede
scene</td>
<td>concrete
precede
convene</td>
<td>kerosene
intervene
centipede</td>
<td>supersede
extremely
discretely
serenely
intercede</td>
<td></td>
<td>e-e</td>
</tr>
</table>

Question: why was the centipede extremely supreme on the trapeze?
Answer: because it has 100 legs.

<table>
<tr>
<td>tree
free
speed
deep
speech
fleet</td>
<td>proceed
degree
beseech
upkeep
decreed</td>
<td>greenhorn
cheetah
leeward
seepage
teeming</td>
<td>addressee
mortgagee
guarantee
employee
jamboree</td>
<td></td>
<td>ee</td>
</tr>
</table>

A referee wanted to meet his committee under a tree or in a tepee or a marquee.
He guaranteed that they could have coffee and toffee at the jubilee if they would
agree.

<table>
<tr>
<td>eat
breathe
beach
eagle
feast
please</td>
<td>eager
easel
teasing
neatly
feature</td>
<td>impeach
displease
repeat
bereave
conceal</td>
<td>cochineal
interweave
misdemeanor
(u) r
predecease
underneath</td>
<td></td>
<td>ea</td>
</tr>
</table>

My Dream Called 'e-a'. In the h**ea**t of summer in my dr**ea**m I l**ea**d a t**ea**m of
b**ea**vers towards a gl**ea**m. They go **ea**st with the stream till they r**ea**ch the s**ea**, so
far ben**ea**th a p**ea**ceful b**ea**ch. They **ea**t m**ea**t and b**ea**ns on a s**ea**t called a b**ea**m.
While one of them sp**ea**ks they have p**ea**ches and cr**ea**m. This tr**ea**t of a m**ea**l, to
say the l**ea**st, would fatten the l**ea**n for it's really a f**ea**st. When filled to the s**ea**ms
they're ever so pl**ea**sed. Then in my dr**ea**m, when going to l**ea**ve, I make b**ea**vers
rep**ea**t that **ea** says /**ee**/ . That's what I t**ea**ch when they're standing at **ea**se: that
ea says /**ee**/, and they think I'm a t**ea**se!

people					**eo**
quay					**ay**
phoenix					**oe**
debris	chassis	verdigris	Louis (d' or)		**is**
encyclopaedia	algae	antennae	formulae	haemoglobin	**ae**
taxi fiord kiosk kiwi suite	medium sardine routine machine serious	champion obedient tangerine serviette previous	convenient experience enthusiastic appropriate immediately		**i**
Sardine was appropriately serious in her suite as she drove the taxi on the previous route.					
baby story handy plenty tidy	memory angry shivery argosy revelry	recovery discovery immunity chivalry eternity	solidarity peculiarity popularity familiarity copyright		**y**
Here's a story of an angry baby who played piano from memory, for eternity.					
key monkey medley barley chutney	lackey motley blarney hackney cockney	hokey-pokey blarney.			**ey**
A medley of the cockney monkey who spoke blarney. Sounds hokey-pokey to me.					
A Sydney jockey on a donkey went on a journey through a valley. He had money in a trolley for hockey in an alley, and a ball game of volley! He saw a chimney on an abbey, a pulley in a two-storey galley, a turkey with some parsley in a kidney, and a monkey in a jersey eating honey with a key.					
ceiling deceive receive receipt	conceive protein	conceivable perceivable	casein caffeine		**ei**

You s**ei**ze your prize as well as the **e** before **i**.
You s**ei**ze prot**ei**n for your health,
You s**ei**ze Mort**ei**n for the flies.

chief brief frieze	Mostly i before e, except after c achieve	achievement hygiene		ie

<u>A Siege</u> A ch**ie**f caught a young th**ie**f in a f**ie**ld. Gr**ie**f changed to rel**ie**f when a misch**ie**vous th**ie**f had to y**ie**ld up his sh**ie**ld to a chief in a f**ie**ld. He was glad to bel**ie**ve in the pr**ie**st's repr**ie**ve.

igloo hint pink grip slid twin	habit digit picnic fillip tipping	optimist minimum criticism prohibit	intimidate diminishing incivility implicitly	invisibility	i

It's the habit of the optimist to have a picnic inside a pink igloo.

pyjamas myth gypsy cygnet system symbol	syrup crystal symptom syringe cymbal	platypus disyllable methylated synonym (ous)	amethyst antonym anonymous metonymy analyst		y

The analyst debunked the myth that the mystic gypsy adorned pyjamas while playing the cymbal; instead, it was the platypus, cloaked in anonymity.

pretty	comedy * tragedy*	privilege barbecue	society		e

In the realm of pretty comedy and tragedy, the privileged unfolds at society barbecue.

sieve					ie
forfeit					ei
forfeit					ei
busy	lettuce	minute			u
build		biscuit circuit			ui

u and i can't build, we must engage a builder.

vehicles	exhibit	exhibitor	exhibition		hi
vehement					he
women					o

i (ice) Sayings its name (long sound)					Sound Group 6
ice violin trial bisect spiral gastritis	spiral compliance inscribing collided appendicitis	arthritis tonsillitis hepatitis meningitis			i
Gastritis, appendicitis, and arthritis, tonsillitis, hepatitis, or meningitis can spiral beyond control.					
pie tie	lie	die	magpie		ie
Magpie would die if it was cooked in a pie.					
	ride wife spike price snipe	oblige polite confide reside	missile	expedite advertise compromise enterprise intertwine	i-e
The wife had a snipe that was not very polite because the advertisement of the ride.					
fly shy pry style type	cyclone pylon xylophone dynamics hypothesis	enzyme analyse paralyse prototype electrolyte	intensify disqualify amplify simplify pacify		y
The hypothesis suggested that it was the flapping of the fly wings that caused the cyclone.					
buy		guy	buying		uy
light righteous	thigh foresight	blight sprightly	upright		igh
I go high to fix the light.					

height	sleight (of hand)				**eigh**
eye					**eye**
dye	sty	goodbye			**ye**
island	isle				**is**
aisle					**ais**
eiderdown	either*	Einstein	kaleidoscope		**ei**
Some people say 'e-ther' and some say i-ther, so put both **e** and **i** when saying either.					

<table>
<tr><td colspan="5">o (orange) Sayings its sound (short sound)</td><td>Sound Group 7</td></tr>
<tr><td>dog
loss
bond
flop
prod
jog</td><td>doctor
sponsor
tosses
poppy
rocking</td><td>lemonade
horology
colonise
mnemonic
harmony</td><td>lollipop
golliwog
apricot
paragon
anthropoid</td><td>rhinoceroses
trigonometry
anthropology
chronology
animosity</td><td>o</td></tr>
<tr><td colspan="6">A mnemonic to help you remember – the doctor of anthropology harmonised the rhinoceroses' animosity with a lollipop.</td></tr>
<tr><td>watch
was
wasp
want
squat</td><td>swallow
washable
squashing
wander</td><td>squadron
squalid
quarrel*
wallow**</td><td>quality
quantity
disqualify
wallaby</td><td></td><td>a</td></tr>
<tr><td colspan="6">Ware a quality watch or watch the wasp.
The wallaby wondered towards the swallow.</td></tr>
<tr><td colspan="6">The / ō / is really ar here. **The / ō / is really al.</td></tr>
<tr><td>Australia
sausage
austere
laurel</td><td>auction
caustic
assault</td><td>cauliflower
hydraulic</td><td></td><td></td><td>au</td></tr>
<tr><td colspan="6">Australians eat a lot of sausage and cauliflower.</td></tr>
<tr><td>cough</td><td colspan="4">trough (see also Letter-Based Groups)</td><td>ou</td></tr>
<tr><td>John</td><td>demijohn</td><td></td><td></td><td></td><td>oh</td></tr>
<tr><td colspan="6">John drank too much wine from the demi-john.</td></tr>
<tr><td>honest
honourable
honesty</td><td>honestly
honorary
honorarium</td><td></td><td></td><td></td><td>ho</td></tr>
<tr><td colspan="6">Honestly you are not honourable, your Honour.</td></tr>
<tr><td>luncheon</td><td>truncheon</td><td></td><td></td><td></td><td>eo</td></tr>
<tr><td>knowledge</td><td>rowlock</td><td></td><td></td><td></td><td>ow</td></tr>
<tr><td>broad</td><td>broadcast</td><td>abroad</td><td></td><td></td><td>oa</td></tr>
</table>

open roll hold post comb	progress coheir go-cart vocal	monogram desolate pantomime envelope	portfolio embargo volcano flamingo	albino	o

It felt like zer**o** by the sil**o**.
A merin**o** listened to the solo.
Was there a banj**o** and pian**o**, or only an alt**o** and soprano?

Just add **s** for the plural.

toe hoe woe	foe floe	oboe throe	mistletoe tiptoe	goes	oe

Woe, under the mistletoe tree, on tiptoe the hoe cut of his toe.

hose code rose drove globe rope	compose microbe promote misquote corrode	microphone telescope episode rigmarole antidote	kaleidoscope anticyclone		o-e

What a rigmarole to promote the telescope instead of the kaleidoscope with a misquote to compose through the microphone.

boat load foam groan soak soap		refloat encroach scapegoat waistcoat bemoan	petticoat overcoat stagecoach cockroach approach	roadworthy unloading soapy gloating toasted	oa

The waistcoated cockroach and the petticoat overcoat sat gloating when they soaked the boat.

snow crow show flow glow tow	rainbow elbow swallow minnow barrow	fellowship narrowing sorrowing widower following	foreshadow overthrow undertow overgrown		ow
The rainbow glowed over the snow but the crow and swallow could not care less.					
owe					ot
depot sabot	robot	haricot (beans etc.)			ot
brooch					oo
plateau tableau trousseau	tonneau	beau tonneau	chateau		eau
All are of French origin.					
oh!					oh
sew					ew
boatswain					oat
yeoman					eo
shoulder	remould				ou
dough	furlough	though	brougham		ough
mould	smoulder	boulder			
Should I shoulder the boulder?					
(see also Letter-Based Groups)					

u (umbrella) Sayings its sound (short sound)					**Sound Group 9**
umbrella up bus fuss junk	puffin subway hubbub	thesaurus stirrup walnut	pendulum nimbus fungus	apparatus hippopotamus auditorium eucalyptus metatarsus	u
The thesaurus really caused the fuss when it published that a hippopotamus arrived at the odditorium in a bus with a hibiscus flower in its metatarsus.					
mother some month front monk tongue (**o-o** -hugs for mother)	money comely colour oven Monday	Among another	wonderful company comfortable covering		o
country (our) couple double trouble	cousin nourish flourish	famous callous spacious	generous coniferous frivolous	ambiguous mountainous ridiculous	ou
It's double trouble to be famous but not generous, quite ridiculous and callous.					
does	(See Building Spelling Cleverness)				oe
flood blood 'Good blood'					oo
cupboard					up
around alive about among	father dance grant	sofa extra comma	vanilla media propaganda		a
Father says that media dogma is propaganda.					

💡 **The sound / ^ / presents many problems. Words ending in us (nouns) or ous (adjectives) may be 'put away' on this page. The sound / A / at the beginning of many words and at the end of most words is spelt a. These words should be put away here, too.**

u (uniform) Sayings its name (long sound)				Sound Group 10
music uniform unit union usurp unite	unicorn unify united universe unison	monument pendulum insulate luxury ambulance	matriculate perpetual meticulous particular perpendicular	u
In the harmonious universe, where melodic music united in a union of symphonic luxury.				
statue due cue sue hue pursue	value issue rescue argue residue	continue revenue barbecue avenue	discontinue undervalue	ue
The value of the statue, you could argue, is due to the barbecue.				
tune cute mute tube fuse mule	confuse transfuse refuge rebuke globule	substitute introduce contribute longitude ridicule	ingratitude redistribute hypotenuse centrifuge superinduce	u-e
Question: What does confuse, and transfuse have in common? Answer: they both have a short fuse.				
queue (long line of boys and girl: **ue ue ue ue**)				ueue
nuisance suitable suitcase	pursuit recruit conduit			ui
'U and I are a nuisance at the dance'.				
adieu	lieu	purlieu		ieu

view preview	review	interview		**iew**
sewerage news hewn stew newt drew	mildew sinew curfew nephew	skewer pewter steward		**ew**
ewe		awe		**ewe**
Euclid feudal euchre feud	neutralise eucalypt eulogy neurosis eurhythmics	pneumonia neurology neutrality pneumatic	Eur…	**eu**
you	youth			**you**
beauty	beautiful	'Be A beaUt, Mum'		**eau**

oo (book) Sayings its sound (short sound) (Note; it is a double vowel)				**Sound Group 11**
book stood crook foot shook	forsook overlook falsehood childhood	goodness footstool tenderfoot neighbourhood		oo
You can read a book, or book and appointment. So, both are homographs.				
could would	should	(See Words in Building Spelling Cleverness)		oul
pull push push(er) bush full bull	pudding pulley pulpit pullet bullet	bushel butcher fulfil (see also Sound Group 25) skilfully		u
Butchers skilfully make bull pudding.				
wolf woman				o

oo (hoop) (Note; it is a double vowel)					**Sound Group 12**
hoop woo scoop(er) groove snooze mood	monsoon teaspoon mushroom festoon whirlpool	nincompoop pantaloon macaroon waterproof	hullabaloo peek-a-boo cockatoo shampoo bamboo		oo

Woo, what fun rolling the hoop until Bandicoot said, "Peek-a-boo" to snoozing Cockatoo. Cockatoo, in a bad mood, called him a nincompoop and threw the teaspoon – this caused a real hullabaloo.

Lose and Loose:
My buttons are loose.(2 buttons,)
Long threads of **o's**. L**os**e a button? L**os**e an **o**.)

rheumatism					eu
to do lode(er) who move*	loser proving mover	undo remove			o

M**o**ve: How many refrigerators could you move? Only one.

shoe	canoe				oe

Sh**o**e: Can't put two **o's**, because you lost one (shoe) and bossy Mum **e** was cross!

two					wo
soup group route wound rouge	routine tourist Louis (d'or)	recoup caribou	cantaloup troubadour		ou

"Can I have cantaloupe soup?" Asked the tourist. "No, but your group can have caribou."

ruler June flute funeral cruel	ruin fluent rumour cruet plural	jubilee survive scrutiny fluency	enthusiastic producing seclusion	jubilantly publication jurisdiction	u
A ruler is an instrument for drawing straight lines and measurements. Or a ruler has jurisdiction over a country. Therefore, both are homographs.					
manoeuvre					oeu
blue cue clue true flue	sue	accrue construe Glue the clue, (blue), to true.	misconstrue		ue
Sue misconstrued the true meaning of the word.					
jewel grew screw drew threw	screwing beshrew	jewellery			ew
through	through (see also Letter-Based Groups,)				ough
fruit sit juice cruise	bruised suitable recruit		You (u) and I like fruit. You and I wear suits. You and I, my dear penguin, not ruin our suits with bruised fruit or juice on the cruise.		ui
pleurisy	rheumatic	rheumatism			eu

					ow
owl howl frown growl clown crowd	drowsy prowler coward trowel rowdy	renown allowed eyebrow sundown endow	glowering allowing empower dowry overpower		

Drowsy Owl, with a frown and a growl was renowned for getting lost in the crowd.

					ou
house (our) our oust cloud bounce sprout	sprouted sounding loutish doubtful mountain	resounding profoundly confounded announcement abounding	greyhound compound aground astound renounce		

Our house is around the corner, the one with the greyhound standing at the gate.

A pr**ou**d m**ou**se went **ou**t r**ou**nd ab**ou**t **ou**r h**ou**se. He f**ou**nd a m**ou**nd of p**ou**nds upon the gr**ou**nd. With his m**ou**th he c**ou**nted them and never made a s**ou**nd. Then a cl**ou**d in the s**ou**th and the sight of a gr**ou**se made him sh**ou**t **ou**t al**ou**d and go off with a b**ou**nd.

hour	hourly				hou

You need a chair(**h**) if you've to wait for an hour.

plough drought	(see also Letter-Based Groups) bough courage				ough

'our' words for faster recall* *based, of course, on spelling, not sound.	on in for see hear notice Mother likes our our	our our our our our our our our our ardour and	age has favourite nourishment eight keys for the out our	honour favour flavour neighbour our behaviour clamour fervour colours court courtesy journey demeanour endeavour	

oy (boy) Sayings its name (long sound)					Sound Group 14
boy toy troy coy joy amoy	boycott oyster royal voyage soy	employment enjoying disloyal flamboyant annoyance	corduroy saveloy viceroy gargoyle		oy
"Oy", with annoyance, shouted the boy "You stole my toy and took my joy."					
coin hoist poise choice quoit join	ointment moisture coinage jointly pointer	avoiding embroider exploiter appointment anointed	hydrofoil counterfoil disembroil maladroit		oi
Ointment for the pain – anointed for the. It was their choice to join them for an appointment by the hydrofoil.					
buoy					uoy

r (rabbit) Sayings its sound (short sound)				Sound Group 15
rabbit drag crest grill trot drain	shrapnel stresses sprinkling shrove-tide scrubbing	pilgrimage outrageous congregate represent description		r
Rabbit has a habit of outrageous representation about the pilgrimage to the congregation.				
parrot berry scurry barrel marrow mirror	error errand torrid terror porridge	terrier porringer sorrowing merrier quarrelling		rr
That parrot is a terrier, quarrelling over the porridge. This is in error as he should be merrier when given the berry.				
write wrap wrench wrist wrath wreck	wrongfully wringing wrinkly wrangler writhing	wretchedness overwrought		wr
You can't write with a wrench. And, the wrangler was overwrought with the wrongfully given sentence.				
rhombus rhyme rhythm	rhubarb rhomboid	rhetoric rheostat rheumatism rhinoceros rhododendron		rh
No, rhubarb does not give the rhinoceros rheumatism. That is just someone's rhetoric.				

ar (car)					Sound Group 16
car star arm dart sharp yard	target partner charter barber harpoon	embargo departed retarded escarpment enlargement	exhilarate oligarchic oviparous patriarch standard		ar

To get to the barber, first depart out of the yard and drive the car with your partner down the escarpment and the target is after a sharp left turn.

galah bah ah	rajah punkah loofah hurrah	verandah Messiah	hallelujah		ah
aunt		**A**unt and **U**ncle (**au**).			au
father task bask bath half grasp	casket fasten pastor pasture psalm	giraffe mirage moustache charade barrage	epitaph raspberry		a

My Father: His **tas**k is to take a **bas**ket to the **cas**tle and to **as**k for a plant in a bath or a **vas**e. My father would rather **fas**ten his calm calf to the palm, but he can't because of the bra**ss** band. He takes his calm calf **fas**t **pas**t a flag at half-ma**st**. At la**st**, for my father a drink of ra**sp**berry in a gla**ss** and he sits on the gra**ss** by the cla**ss**.

are	Bossy Mum says, "Where are you?"				are
heart hearth	hearty hearken				ear
clerk		sergeant			er

nougat					at
bazaar	The ba**zaar** was bi**zarr**e.				aar
bizarre					arre
catarrh					arrh

er					Sound Group 17
flower pershower timber bumper	clever number cloister her flower	person sermon fertile perplex perfect persuade	emperor observer funeral federal sorcerer	unilateral probationer upholsterer collateral supervisor recuperate	er

Clever person taking a flower to the funeral to give to the number one supervisor. That was perfect, and just before you went into the cloister.

transferred preferred referred					err
learn search yearn pearl hearse heard	earnest earldom earthward earthen earthquake	rehearsal earthliness earnestly searchingly			ear

I heard if you yearn for learning and rise early to search earnestly and rehearse at each rehearsal, you earn pearls on earth.

were	'we were'				ere
fire lyre tyre hire theatre	acre fibre sombre meagre conspire	umpire perspire retire transpire massacre	kilometre manoeuvre calibre mediocre		re

An umpire officiates the game, players perspire, and dreams retire as stories transpire.

The Ogre Fire:

There was a fire by a theatre.

Tyres were on fire in the centre of an acre of land.

Firemen were desired and hired: they were inspired, admired.

Police were required at the fire to enquire. They were all tired, of the ogre fire.

bird sir fir skirt twirl mirth	astir bestir	skirmish chirping smirking	elixir respiration aspirin affirmative aspiration		**ir**

Birds and Circles Look! A nest, **fir**m in a **fir** tree. Mother **bird** circles, baby **bird**s chirp, Mother **bird**stirs and st**ir**s, baby **bir**ds whirl, swirl and twirl. First **bird** sits on a sh**ir**t. Next one stands on a sk**ir**t, Third one settles on d**ir**t. What m**ir**th! They all find water that squ**ir**ts. Squ**ir**t the **dir**ty bird. All are ast**ir**, the g**ir**l and s**ir**. Birds and c**ir**cles.

martyr	satyr zephyr	martyr			**yr**
myrrh					**yrrh**
collar* pillar solar dollar standard	farther orchard drunkard harbor	circular infirmary nearest			**ar**

The sound is usually, of course, indefinite. The words should be put away under sound: either here or with Sound Group 16 (**ar**).

world worm worse worth work worst	worship wordy doctor motor pallor		foreword catchword watchword		**or**

a conductor (a bus conductor or an orchestral conductor?) said to the doctor, "Your work is worth mirroring.

journey	courage journal courteous	labourer candour colour valour favour			**our***

We journalised with candour, and some colour, of the valour of our favourite and courteous labourer.

See also Sound Group 20 / ɔ / pronunciation preferred for colour. * Letter-Based Groups or more words using clue 'our'.					
colonel					olo
church surf urge purse curl lurk	sturdy further survey Thursday surgeon	disturb murmur outburst upsurge unfurl	reimburse survivors urgently nursery pursuers		ur

On Thursday the survivors wanted to know do they go and surf or go to the church?

I take my purse on purpose, to pursue the thing I want to purchase.

| purr
burr | demurred
furry | occurred | | | urr |

The furry cat purred.

| figure
conjure
fissure | disfigure
leisure | | | | ure |

The figure became disfigured because when on leisure it fell down the fissure.

air					Sound Group 18	
chair stair flair fair pair lair	**and** i bun to... dairy hairy fairy despair repair	impair eclair mohair unfair affair	disrepair debonair repairing despairing			air

A pair of f**air** haired d**air**y boys sat on a ch**air**. They fell down the st**air**s and were in desp**air** for they couldn't rep**air**
the ch**air**. What an aff**air**! Until a f**air**y came out of her l**air** and did the rep**air**. (She had a fl**air** for rep**air**!)

| scarecrow
flare
spare
square
fare
beware | warfare
ensnare
outdare
nightmare | declare
declare
prepare | earthenware
thoroughfare
unaware
threadbare
ploughshare | | | are |

C**ar**, take c**are**! St**ar**, don't st**are**! Go f**ar**, pay a f**are**. On the b**ar**, feet b**are**. Only a sc**ar**, no sc**are**! Do not sp**ar**, please sp**are**.
Do not m**ar** your m**are**. I'm aw**are** a r**are** h**are** d**are**s gl**are** at sc**are**crows. I decl**are** he said in the sq**uare** just to sh**are** and comp**are** the w**are**s prepared. Take c**are**! Take a boss (e), to drive a c**ar** with c**are**.

millionaire	questionnaire	commissionaire				aire
Mary vary wary		scaring glaring sparing	preparing comparing declaring	vegetarian octogenarian		ar

Contra**ry** Ma**ry** is w**ary**, and does not v**ary**. She's c**ar**ing and sp**ar**ing and d**ar**ing,

| bear
tear
pear
wear | outwear
outswear
bugbear | overbearing
forebare
forbearance | | | | ear |

A b**ear** eats a p**ear** and t**ear**s the clothes he w**ear**s.

where	there				ere
their	heir				eir
prayer					ayer

mayor					**ayor**
aeroplane	aerial	aerodrome	aerobatics		**aer**

eer (Note it is a double vowel)					Sound Group 19
deer steer jeer	cheer steering peerage deerhound seersucker	sneer veneer career overseer volunteer	profiteer auctioneer domineer mountaineer		**eer**

The D**eer** and the Engin**eer**: An engin**eer** will volunt**eer** to pion**eer** and be a mountain**eer**. He'll ch**eer** the d**eer** and st**eer** the d**eer** if
they have b**eer** and begin to car**eer** as if they are agree. He will not sh**eer** nor be a mutin**eer**. This engin**eer** will be a s**eer**, a pion**eer**.

ear	earmark	appear	disappearance		**ear**
ear clear spear rear smear year	earmark earwig tearful fearsome gearbox	appear arrears endear besmear headgear	disappearance overhearing endearment endearingly		

here	Doctor, I'm sinc**ere**. The pain is sev**ere** here and it's m**ere**ly a sph**ere** but I'll persev**ere** if you don't interf**ere** with the atmosph**ere**!				**ere**

cereal	serial	inferior	stereotype		**er**
cereal era hero zero Nero	serial serum period serious	inferior exterior superior	stereotype		

pier		cashier	chandelier	fusilier	**ier**
pier fierce frontier pierce bier		cashier gondolier chiffonier fiercest	chandelier cavalier	fusilier	

On the pier the fierce gondolier, back from the frontier stood by the bier with a tear in his eyes.

weir	weird	weirdly			**eir**
souvenir					**ir**

or					Sound Group 20
horse horn cord form born lord	forward mortal fortune torment dormant	remorse forlorn abhor corridor metaphor	assortment subordinate extortion disorderly scorpion		or

| sore
more
chore
score
lore
fore | foreshore
foresight
forecast
forego
scorer | encore
fourscore
explore
ignore
therefore | stevedore
pinafore
commodore
semaphore
sycamore | | ore |

More About **S**ore and Bob: This boy Bob did his mother ad**ore**, yet mother's advice did Bob ign**ore**, for he wanted to go to the sh**ore** to expl**ore**. The shoes Bob w**ore**, alas, they t**ore**! He went to the st**ore** with feet so s**ore**, for plasters gal**ore** he did impl**ore**, but m**ore** and m**ore** Bob did deplore bef**ore** his feet he could rest**ore**!

| oar
soar
hoarse
hoard
coarse
boar | | boarder
hoarded
hoarseness
roaring
coarsely | surfboard
uproar
cardboard
cupboard
starboard | uproarious
coarseness
oarsmanship | oar |

| mortgage | | | | | ort |

After their mournful behaviour they endeavoured to pour the entire fourteen thousand into the mortgage.

| pour
four
mourn
course
court | fourteen
mournful
coursing
courtly | splendour*
humour
glamour
saviour | (mis)behaviour
(dis)honour
endeavour
(mis)
demeanour | | our |

Floorwalker Joe opened the door to check the new floor. He thought the quality very poorly done.

*See also Sound Group 17, our if / **er** / pronunciation is preferred for the words in the last two columns.					
door floor poorly poor boor	doorstep outdoor mooring flooring	boorishness indoor	floorwalker moor		**oor**
sure surely	insure	insurance			**ur**
You've had a fire, so you (**U**) rush everywhere to be sure to insure the property and assure the future					
thought ought	bought brought	thoughtful	thoughtfulness		**ough**
I thought they said, "oh, you go home!" (**o-u-g-h**)					

paw claw thaw lawn sprawl squawk	awful awkward awning lawyer trawler	rickshaw outlaw pawpaw withdraw seesaw		aw
Yes, there is an awful claw on the paw. But is it a paw or a pawpaw?				
awe	awesome			awe
auntie & uncle (autumn) automatic auditorium				au
You had to sweep up the autumn leaves because auntie and uncle were coming for tea. They like sauce with their meal.				
fault jaunt taunt flaunt staunch	laundry saunter autumn cautious augment austere	defaulting assaulted applauding tarpaulin thesaurus precaution	plausibility authenticity nautical	au
In autumn without precaution to jaunt, taunt and flaunt with little caution.				
war swarm dwarf warp wharf quart	reward forewarn award towards awkward	warder warbling thwarted quarterly	enthralled forestalling recalled	ar
the dwarf on the wharf was awarded a reward from the war.				
wall chalk waltz squall bald	almost also already alter although	walrus scalded walnut instalment		a(1)

My clue is all. What do I do to all to make all say bald or waltz, or halter or scald? I'll end with salt, but you must not halt till you know about all because all can talk.				
caught taught haughty	naughty daughter	slaughter		augh
Naughty daughter, caught in the slaughter.				
dinosaur minotaur				aur
exhaust exhaustion				hau
water				a

k (i) Sayings its sound (short sound)					Sound Group 21
kitten skin task keg sank **k** is for silky kitten skin.	skipper skittish kelpie sketchy skewer	casket trinket turkey silky hawking	musketeer handkerchief murkiness kerosene skeleton		k
cake spike choke duke	pancake rebuke provoke turnpike earthquake	artichoke undertake ladylike overtake wide-a-wake			ke

Wide-a-wake and ladylike until she'd choked on the artichoke. This provoked the servant to offer a pancake, but her rebuke is like an earthquake.

walk chalk talk	folk yolk				(l) k
khaki khan	khedive	gymkhana			kh
trekked					kk
queen squib quest quiz quell quote	require liquid frequent request inquire	qualify quality quandary squanderer squeamishness	inquisitive requisite acquisition acquaintance frequency		q

The student said, "To quote our queen: to qualify in your quest for the quiz, requires frequent quality of homework.

quoits quay quoin	marquee liquor	mosquito liquorice conqueror	mannequin etiquette masquerade		qu

At the quay the mosquito, masquerading as a mannequin, drunk the liquor and ate the liquorice.

| cheque
mosque
plaque
pique
brusque | opaque
unique
oblique
antique | grotesque
physique
technique
burlesque | picturesque
humoresque | | que |

With a grotesque physique derived from the plague, the doctor with a picturesque and unique technique operated in the mosque to save the patients.

cat cog cup cart cash camel	escape locate coconut cactus crocus	cascaded percolate conclusive incorrect reconstruct	cavalcade lubricate nautical massacre ct medical	ecstatic statistic acoustic Antarctic characteristic	c

c for cat, and c for cactus and camel sound like they could be **k** for kitten.

account occur hiccough succedent accordion	accurate moccasin occasion	tobacco Morocco impeccable	Malacca accommodate occasional		cc

Tobacco accounted for the occasional hiccups to occur in that accommodation in Morocco. Not in Malacca as you thought.

duck track crock tick pluck sack	picket reckless tackling knick-knack rocket	padlock matlock attack cassock limerick	mackintosh acknowledge backwardness mackerel checkmate		ck

Ducks and mackerel don't need a macintosh to keep them dry.

school ache choir chasm echo chord Christmas	chorus chemist scholar chaotic chronic	chloroform chiropractor chiropodist chrysalis chronicle	orchestra anarchist archaic synchronize architecture		ch

The school's Christmas chorus still echoes in the ear of the chiropractor.

Children go to school. There they sing in the choir.

acquire acquit acquaint	acquiesce acquaintance	acquisitive			cq

racquet	lacquer				cqu
		95			
saccharine Bacchus	bacchant	bacchanalian			cch

<table>
<tr><td colspan="5">k Sayings its name (long sound)</td><td>Sound Group 22</td></tr>
<tr><td>snakes
sash
spats
stilts
socks
sets</td><td>suspect
sister
spinster
sponsor
escape</td><td>subsidy
distrust
resistance
subsistence
subscription</td><td>synthesis
stethoscope
synopsis
metamorphosis
thrombosis</td><td></td><td>s</td></tr>
<tr><td colspan="6">Snakes don't wear socks when they escape on stilts. But sometimes they carry a stethoscope to diagnose the thrombosis.</td></tr>
<tr><td>case
tense
chase
glimpse</td><td>expanse
eclipse</td><td>universe
intersperse</td><td>hypotenuse
apocalypse</td><td></td><td>se</td></tr>
<tr><td colspan="6">a case can be used for carrying things. Or there can be a case at the courthouse in response to the apocalypse.</td></tr>
<tr><td colspan="6">I'm dense if I forget that immense expense creates intense suspense and makes no sense or nonsense.</td></tr>
<tr><td>dress
miss
cross
fuss
ass
puss</td><td>assess
address
emboss
hostess
distress</td><td>dismissal
embarrassing
retrogressive
predecessor
repossessing</td><td>indistinctness
outspokenness
defencelessness
characterless</td><td>Possess
possesses
two double
sses.</td><td>ss</td></tr>
<tr><td colspan="6">"Assess the dress of your predecessor," said the hostess.</td></tr>
<tr><td>sword</td><td>answer</td><td>swordfish</td><td>swordsman</td><td></td><td>sw</td></tr>
<tr><td colspan="6">"Swing your sword." or your sword is your word!</td></tr>
<tr><td>listen
castle
trestle
gristle
jostle</td><td>rustling
wrestling
whistling
bristling</td><td>epistle
fasteners
moistening
listener</td><td>chastening
christening
glistening</td><td></td><td>st</td></tr>
<tr><td colspan="6">The Epistle chastised the christening for people whistling near the trestle by the castle wall where they also jostled and bustled. But no one listened to him.</td></tr>
</table>

bustle isthmus	mistletoe	hastening			**sth**
psalm psychic	psalmist	psoriasis	psychology psychopath		**ps**
crevasse finesse	impasse lacrosse	palliasse			**sse**

					c(e)
cent, fence space since force dunce bounce	accept receive precede recent decent	certificate cenotaph cemetery censorship centimetre	reinforce precipice introduce frontispiece mispronounce		

Beyond the cemetery fence there is space to receive a decent frontispiece.

					c(i)
city, pencil cinder cider circus cinch circuit	council acid concise precise decide	incinerator incidental incipient civilian civility	germicide exercise suicide coincide convincing		

"Fancy a cycle on the bicycle?" With diplomacy, the cyclist replied cynically. "Have mercy on me for the legacy of his piracy."

					c(y)
cycle, tricycle cygnet cymbal cyclist fancy mercy scythe	cyclamen cyanide cylinder cynosure cynical	bicycle tricycle supremacy encyclical encyclopaedia	diplomacy pharmacy piracy legacy		

The scythe and crescent are reminiscent of the same shape.

					sc
scenery scent science		descend rescind crescent transcend	oscillate condescend plebiscite quiescent	effervescent phosphorescent reminiscent	
convalesce reminisce effervesce	acquiesce fluoresce coalesce	phosphoresce incandesce			sce

Problem Letter Combinations

					cess
princess necessary access process	excess success	intercession predecessor			

Intercession isn't necessary for the princess' success. There is already a process to access this.					
busy 'ence' * learn Sound Group 5 'ense' and call everything else busy 'ence'					ence
occurrence					ance

					g
gun	fragrant	omega	Gorgonzola		
gag	progress	monogram	gargantuan		
gang	gargoyle	flamingo	mahogany		
grip	magnet	gelignite	obligation		
glebe	pentagon	gregarious			
engulf					

The Pentagon has a gargoyle and a gregarious flamingo as a monogram.

				gg
trigger	stagger	struggling	bedraggled	
giggle	goggles	braggart	outrigger	
waggle	luggage	lagging	doggedly	
juggle	gagging	maggot	raggedly	
wriggle				

Giggle and wriggle sang the bedraggled maggot doggedly.

					gu
guide		guitar	beguile	guillotine	
guy		guiltless	disguise	guarantee	
guest*		guiltless	safeguard	guerilla	
guild		Guernsey	rearguard	guardian	
guard		gunea			

Special work on **gues**s: **gues**sed, **gues**t and **ques**t.

					gh
ghost	gherkin	aghast	ghostliness		
ghat	ghetto	dinghy			
ghee	ghastly				
	gharry				
	ghazi				

Ghastly ghosts ate ghee and gherkin in my dingy.

				gue
plague	intrigue	dialogue	pedagogue	
rogue	fatigue	monologue		
vague	prologue	catalogue		
morgue	colleague	epilogue		
league	synagogue			
vogue				

It is in the vogue to monologue a vague dialogue as the epilogue to the story.

J for jug; j for major				**Sound Group 24**	
jug jest jam jig	jacket jerky jingle junket	banjo conjure major prejudice	justify janitor juvenile jaguar	disjointed conjunction conjuror bubbly-jock	j

The janitor said, "There is jam in the jug.

cage change gent large genius general	gentle Gentile ginger pigeon gorgeous	merger anchorage sergeant pageantry engagement	vegetarian submerged subterfuge sewerage		g(e)

The gorgeous pigeon ate in the cage.

giraffe giant gift gibber ginger	fragile raging digit rigid	regiment agility regional agitate	vigilance tragically agitation gigantic	strategist geologist psychologist archaeologist	g(i)

The gigantic neck of the giraffe is fragile said the archaeologist to the psychologist with agitation.

gym gypsum gyre gymnast gyrate	bulgy clergy spongy dingy	gymnasium gymkhana gyroscope strategy	ecology eulogy effigy ecology		g(y)

The gymnast prodigy had a strategy to gyrate at the gymkhana.

suggest					gg

bridge budget lodger gadget ledger judge	porridge partridge abridged dislodged adjudged	fledgeling hedgehog cudgelling drudgery bludgeon	foreknowledge acknowledge misjudgement hodge-podge		**dge**
A ju**dge** sat behind a he**dge** on the e**dge** of a le**dge** by the ri**dge** of the bri**dge**. He ate porri**dge** with knowle**dge**.					
(mi**dge**t, le**dge**r, fi**dge**t, ba**dge**r: see above, **dge**)					**dg**
adjust adjoin adjourn adjunct	adjective adjacent adjutant	adjustment adjournment readjustment			**dj**
"Let us adjourn and adjust the program."					
soldier "I sold my soldier."					**di**

I (contrary)					Sound Group 25
full	fulfil				fill
skill true truly whole wholly (role, hole)	skilful skilfully slowly gradually beautifully				full
Gradually, he gained truly beautiful skill.					
roll	unroll	enrol control patrol	enrolled controlling patrolled	enrolment	roll
Enrolled to control the patrol.					
tell	retell	excel travel jewel rebel	excellent traveller jewellery rebellious		tell
I tell you it was excellent jewellry.					
Short words, two l's, but longer words lose an l, add some more, add an l.					
all at the end of words:		**mostly all l's, sometimes one l**			-all
		recall	pall appal	install (-ing) instal (-ment)	
all at the beginning of words:		**making one word, one l**			al-
Always, well almost, we alternate the altar, as that is how it is written in the almanac.					
almost already altar	almighty altogether alteration	almanac always alternate	although (see Letter-Based Groups)		
all as a separate word (non-compound word):					all
		all right	all wrong		

tranquil distil instil					**il**
wilful hopeful grateful wasteful harmful watchful	dutiful merciful beautiful	purposeful remorseful distasteful reproachful disdainful wonderful			**ful**
Tis wasteful to be disdainful – rather be dutiful and merciful.					
gambol carol extol					**ol**
Carol is a girl's name and the name of a Christmas song.					
tunnel channel shrivel bevel	level shovel marvel swivel repel	unravel counsel dishevel			**el**
The correct tunnel is one level above.					

lamp flannelette geniality vandalism	venality vigilant civility	symbolise paralleled		**l**

To stop vandalism you must be vigilant.

parallel				**ll**

elephant celery elegance elevator celebrate	delegate skeleton elect elegy	elect electric electricity accelerate		**(ele)**

Celebrate the elephant's elegance.

colony colossal biology theology dolomite	apology geology solo(ist) galosh Solomon	symbologist phraseology pharmacologist meteorology	polo polonaise	**(olo)**

In the colony geology is taught as part of theology.

balance salad salary valance	stalactite avalanche			**(ala)**

agility ability vilify silica	gentility civility military militant	nobility servility		**(ili)**

Her agility and ability are full of gentility civility.

candle twinkle angle table	gamble gentle dangle	trample sample simple		**le**

It is a gamble to let the candle dangle on the table edge unsupervised.

camel angle travel counsel novel swivel morsel	The Colonel: A colon**el** wearing flann**el** from a barr**el** shov**el**s grav**el**. On a camel trav**el**s lev**el** with an ang**el** in a parc**el**. He finds jew**el**s and a tow**el** in a funn**el** by a tunn**el**, and this colon**el** wearing flann**el** never quarr**el**s with his cam**el**.			**el**
animal annual local central	original nominal			**al**
The local annual animal show is in Central city.				
pencil stencil civil council	civil April	The small pencil represents the i, and the large penc**il** represents the l.		**il**
carol petrol symbol gambol idol				**ol**
The idol sang the carol.				
gazellebelle	Moselle			**lle**

f for fish; f for forty Sayings its sound (short sound)				Sound Group 26	
fish fluff fifty flip fox	fifth forty favour finger	reproof engulf herself twelfth	unfairly disfavour disfigure profusion	waterproof misbelief overleaf handkerchief*	f
Fox unfairly ate the fish himself.					
knife safe chafe	housewife vouchsafe				fe
The housewife is safe using the knife. I can vouchsafe for that.					
coffee fluff cuff* staff cliff	offer offence riffraff bluff	sheriff tariff plaintiff handcuff	officer ruffian raffia rebuffed	effective effeminate affirmative affected*	ff
The sheriff rebuffed the offer of coffee for his staff.					
giraffe					ffe
phone phlox photo phonics phantom phase	orphan hyphen siphon dolphin typhoon	pharmacy physical philosophy phenomenon philanthropist	cenotaph epitaph telegraph cardiograph catastrophe		ph
She told me on the phone that without this phonics phase, it would be a catastrophe.					

rough tough cough laugh draught	laughter tougher coughed roughage	draughtsman toughened coughing roughness	enough laughing roughened		**gh**
The draughtsman coughed after being in the draught.					
soften	often	oftener	softener		**ft**
half halfpenny halfwit	calfskin	halfback	behalf		**lf**
The halfwit played halfback.					
lieutenant					**u**
sapphire	sapphirine				**pph**
* Plurals:	The **chief** 's handker**chief**s blew from the roof to the cliffs.				

<table>
<tr><td colspan="5">v Sayings its sound (short sound)</td><td>Sound Group 27</td></tr>
<tr><td>van
valve
velvet
oven
seven
vacant</td><td>clover
haven
liver
quaver
proven</td><td>violin
violent
visible
volatile</td><td>eleven
enliven
envisage
survival
dissolve</td><td></td><td>v</td></tr>
<tr><td colspan="6">The seven violins are wrapped in velvet and are not visible in the back of the van.</td></tr>
<tr><td>twelve
loaves*
shelves
dove
stove
pave
delve
twelve</td><td>captive
involve
revive
motive
active
absolve
resolve
involve
dissolve</td><td>detective
objective
secretive
tentative
positive</td><td>locomotive
primitive
competitive
inquisitive
inattentive</td><td></td><td>ve</td></tr>
<tr><td colspan="6">Twelve doves tentatively perched on the shelves.</td></tr>
<tr><td>halves*
calves
salve</td><td></td><td></td><td></td><td></td><td>(1)

ve</td></tr>
<tr><td>of</td><td></td><td></td><td></td><td></td><td>f</td></tr>
<tr><td>nephew</td><td>Stephen</td><td></td><td></td><td></td><td>ph</td></tr>
<tr><td>* -ves
plurals:</td><td colspan="5">'olves and thieves steal loaves from wharves.</td></tr>
</table>

th (voiceless)					Sound Group 28	
three thrill thin thing throng thank	fifth sixth twelfth tenth width	path length heath wreath thermometer	thirteenth thirtieth diphthong ophthalmia	3		th
th (voiced)						th
clothes this then than thou those these them	thus thine there theirs therefore though	bathe other thither whither tether heather	scythe clothe			

Last **Thursday they thought** that **Thor threw thunder** at the **thief** over **there. This** time, **though,** I **th**ink he **thr**eatened to **thr**ow **three thousand thorny thistles** at **those** o**the**r **th**irsty, **thieving thugs.**

sh (1)					Sound Group 29
ship shade shed shop shut shy	finish relish selfish varnish refresh	worshipped dishevelled brandished publisher polisher	diminish admonish extinguish impoverish macintosh		**sh**

Varnish the ship's floors and finish with the polisher admonished Mr McIntosh, who selfishly stood in the shade refreshed.

cushion	fashion	fashionable			**shi**

It's the fa**shion** to have a cu**shion** in the car.

extension mansion pension version tension	expansion extension dimension expulsion	comprehension apprehension condescension			**si**

pressure	assurance	reassuringly			**ss**

Pressure was reassuringly applied.

discussion mission fission	possession confession admission omission	expression concession obsession concussion	impression profession permission compression		**ssi**

There was a discussion to ask for permission to go onto the mission.

unconscious conscious luscious	conscionable conscience	impression profession permission compression			**sci**

Surely, you must be conscientious about eating too much sugar.

sugar sure	surely surely	insure insurance			**s**

composition mention action auction patient motion	invention prevention venetian Alsatian fictitious	examination explanation indication publication dedication	fabrication humiliation specification personification confidential		**ti**
Don't men**ti**on the composi**ti**on!					
musician special social spacious gracious precious	commercial tenacious audacious precocious optician	inefficient insufficient coefficient beneficiary electrician			**ci**
Our precocious musician has a special routine before commercial performances, unlike her social outings.					
ocean cetacean	herbaceous	crustacean	cetacean		**ce**
Crustaceans live in the ocean, so they are not herbaceous.					
machine chef chute chaise chagrin	chalet charade chamois chateau champagne	machine crochet ricochet parachute	chandelier char-a-banc chivalry		**ch**
At the chalet the chef opened the champagne when the machine had finished.					
moustache					**che**
anxious noxious	inflexion luxury (see Letter-Based Groups)				**xi**

ch				**Sound Group 30**
chop chin chart choke check impeachment	chapter Chinese chiming chisel entrenched	ostrich spinach vouch detach detachment	chinchilla cochineal mischievous surcharge handkerchief	ch
You chop to cut something. Or a chop is eaten.				
match ditch clutch	sketch crutch switch	hitch-hike ketchup	slapstick hopscotch	tch
Can you match slapstick hopscotch they performed?				
question digestion combustion	indigestion exhaustion suggestion			ti
"The question is, was it indigestion or exhaustion that made you retire?"				
cello	cellist			c

<table>
<tr><td colspan="4">t Sayings its sound (short sound)</td><td></td><td>Sound Group 31</td></tr>
<tr><td>top
tart
test
tint
tuft
tot</td><td>tactful
talent
tasty
tantrum
textile</td><td>tentative
testator
tale-teller
tantamount
tripartite</td><td>inconsistent
omnipotent
incompetent
impertinent
entertainment</td><td></td><td>t</td></tr>
<tr><td colspan="6">The entertainers were top talent.</td></tr>
<tr><td>gate
route
kite
mote</td><td>granite
senate
private
devote</td><td>opposite
composite
destitute</td><td>investigate
substituted
instituting</td><td></td><td>te</td></tr>
<tr><td colspan="6">Please investigate the senate's opposition in helping the destitute.</td></tr>
<tr><td>button
watt
butt
putt
cattle
kettle</td><td>tattoo
lettuce
cotton
gutted
twitter</td><td>permitted
committee
regretting
forgotten
boycotting</td><td></td><td></td><td>tt</td></tr>
<tr><td colspan="6">A tattoo is permitted by the committee.</td></tr>
<tr><td>intersect
indict
abstract
victim
verdict</td><td colspan="3">You don't really hear the c, but you hear a pause, so put a letter.</td><td></td><td>ct</td></tr>
<tr><td>debt
doubt</td><td>subtle
debtor
doubtless</td><td>subtlety
It's bad to be in debt.</td><td></td><td></td><td>bt</td></tr>
<tr><td>receipt</td><td>You'll get one when you Pay.</td><td></td><td></td><td></td><td>pt</td></tr>
<tr><td>yacht</td><td>yachting
yachtsman
I want to
say ya-ch-t
!</td><td>yachtsmanship</td><td></td><td></td><td>cht</td></tr>
</table>

					tte
cigarette gazette gavotte	cassette palette burette pipette	brunette omelette	flannelette serviette		
The brunette had a cigarette after her omelette whilst reading the gazette.					
thyme	thymic	Thomas			th
veldt					dt
chopped	See Sound Group 39, d at the end of words.				ed

z Sayings its name (long sound)					Sound Group 32
zoo zoom zone zero zinc zeal	quiz waltz fez whiz quartz	zebra zephyr zither z zany crazy	breezy frenzy wizard lazy zeppelin	zinnia zodiac zealously zoology	z
In the zoo the crazy zebra did a waltz with zeal.					
prize craze size maize	trapeze capsize amaze	capsizable amazement sneezeweed	criticise minimise syllabize		ze
Don't capsize or criticize or you will not receive the prize. N.B; US spelling.					
glaze	ablaze	breezeway	ostracise		
For the above these are both US and UK Spelling puzzle buzz jazz fizz muzzle	guzzled embezzle bedazzle razzle-dazzle	sizzling drizzly buzzard grizzly	frizziness grizzlier mezzanine embezzlement		zz
At the jazz club there was a buzz because of the razzle-dazzle.					
logs posy pansy spasm chasm	posies cosmos houses browses	residuals provisos fiascos dynamos	antagonism euphemism euthanasia microcosm		s
A pretty posy of a pansy and cosmos.					

					se
rose fuse vise these surprise	noise phrase ease	surmise disused refused	diagnose analyse paraphrase hypotenuse		

A rose can be a flower and a girl's name.

A Japanese vase with a painted rose.

scissors	dissolve	possession			ss
boy's toys					's
xylophone	xenophobia,				x

zh				Sound Group 33
measure treasure pleasure closure leisure erasure	enclosure disclosure composure exposure			s
Measure how far the treasure is in the back of the enclosure.				
television invasion evasion fusion	provision collision adhesion intrusion incision conclusion	occasion division precision persuasion illusion supervision		si
With supervision the children can occasionally watch television.				

			Sound Group 34
yacht yard yak youth year	yellow yodel youngest youthful		y
The youth scrutinised yellow yacht in back of the demolition yard.			
onion union junior million billion	pinion valiant brilliant stallion		i
Union rules state that juniors must not eat onions.			
Jugoslav	hallelujah,		j

					w
web well wet wind wag	wither winter wagon wallet	shadowy arrowroot yellowfish safflower	foreshadow disavow bungalow overthrow		

The safflower withered in the winter cold.

					u
quick quilt quack quest quite suite suave	quarterly quadrangle quality quadruped suede anguish dissuade	inquiry liquify inquisitive language persuade assuage suasion	consequently subsequent delinquent iniquitous sanguine languish		

The quarterly inquiry is being held in the quadrangle. Our quest is to dissuade the delinquent of the consequences of her actions.

					u
choir	boudoir memoir coiffure	shadowy arrowroot yellowfish safflower	foreshadow		

The choir sang as part of the memoir.

					wh
wheel when where whiff whip which	whine white while whale whirl	whimper whitening whisper whipping whatever	wheeze whisker whenever wharf		

Don't whine whenever the whale passes away from the wharf.

					m
man	member	remember	memorandum		
mop	mimic	immemorial	momentum		
mum	moment	dismember	optimism		
mint	mumbling	anemometer	pessimism		
mesh	memoir		minimum		
mate					

The man's mate was mumbling through the memoir because of the mint sweet in his mouth. He said, "Remember his mum was a member of the club."

				mm
hammer	mammal	persimmon		
drummer	mammoth	commandeer		
swimming	summon	commiserate		
stammer	common	commission		
summer	gimmick			
hemming				

The drummer commiserated with the swimmer's stammer. It is a common complaint.

					me
game	sublime	timely	pantomime		
grime	presume	homestead	maritime		
fame	inflame	sameness	metronome		
tome	perfume	shameful	aerodrome		
fume					

The pantomime was in the metronome, adjacent to the aerodrome.

				em
emblem	system			
	problem			
	anthem			

					mb
lamb	succumb	honeycomb			
limb	benumb	disentomb			
comb	entomb	catacomb			
crumb	coxcomb	aplomb			
climb					

Lamb and limb – silent e.

					mn
autumn	condemn				
hymn	solemn				
damn	column				

Damn the autumn hymn.

blossom bottom wisdom fathom venom custom.	freedom kingdom symptom seldom				**om**
a word of wisdom – you can blossom with freedom					
palm calm balm qualm	psalm salmon psalmist qualmish	becalm embalm			**lm**
Palms are trees. Psalms are songs of praise.					
program	(programme)	See USA/UK Spelling list In the Extra Mastery Page.			**mme**
phlegm	diaphragm epiphragm				**gm**

					n
nest nun ninth none neon	nineteenth nonsense contend canine	nonagon banana dependent enhance	nonconformist nonagenarian nomination genuine		

The nun thought it nonsense that none of the bananas were left. To contend with this, she lit frankincense. Don't get confused between nun and none.

					nn
dinner inn Finn pennant tonnage	manner shinning	antennae perennial unannounced	reconnaissance annotation disconnection annuitant		

What's for dinner at the inn?

					kn
knife knot knee know knight knoll	knapsack knowledge knighthood knitting knocking	knowledgeable knicker-bockers acknowledging unknowingly			

When you hike up the knoll you need a knife in your knapsack.

The **kn**owledgeable **kn**ight **kn**ows about **kn**aves and **kn**ackers who **kn**it **kn**ickerbockers and **kn**ock their **kn**obbly **kn**ees when **kn**eeling, begging to the cook **kn**eading dough with a **kn**ife and her **kn**uckles for bread to fill their **kn**apsacks before **kn**otting them.

					gn
gnaw gnat gnash gnome gnu gnaw	gnomic gnosis gnarled gnawing	gnashing gnomon			

The **gn**ome **gn**ashed his teeth at the **gn**at **gn**awing the **gn**u.

					pn
pneumonia	pneumatic				

					dne
Wednesday					

					nd
grandpa	sandwich	grandma			

| mnemonics | | | | | mn |
| epergne | champagne | eau-de-Cologne | | | gne |

<table>
<tr><td colspan="5">n (near the end of the words)
</td><td></td></tr>
<tr><td>engine
shone
none
pine
one
done</td><td>vaccine
benzine
cocaine
sardine
quinine</td><td>imagine
examine
determine
discipline
genuine</td><td>quarantine
tangerine
caffeine
heroine</td><td></td><td>ne</td></tr>
</table>

Our heroine thank you drove the engine with genuine discipline.

<table>
<tr><td>chicken
golden
deafen
smarten</td><td>worsen
freshen</td><td>enlighten
citizen
dishearten</td><td>overburden
shortening</td><td>moisten
listen
soften</td><td>en</td></tr>
</table>

Behold the citizens of Global Chicken land. Do not be disheartened, or frightened, we must continue with our work to enlighten.

<table>
<tr><td>elephant
thousand
garland</td><td>brigand
Shetland</td><td>England</td><td></td><td></td><td>an</td></tr>
</table>

if a thousand elephants went to England, England would sink into the ocean.

<table>
<tr><td>curtain
boatswain
coxswain
chaplain
bargain</td><td>Britain
captain
certain
villain</td><td>porcelain
chamberlain
mountainous</td><td></td><td></td><td>ain</td></tr>
</table>

I'm cert**ain** no capt**ain** needs a curt**ain** up a mount**ain**.
No capt**ain** wants to barg**ain** with a vill**ain** by a fount**ain**.

<table>
<tr><td>lion
dragon
ribbon
tendon</td><td>common
summon
python</td><td>religion
imprison
jettison</td><td>comparison
orpington</td><td></td><td>on</td></tr>
</table>

Lily Lion ate Peter Python, who in turn was eaten by the Freddy Falcon. He thought it just like mutton.

basin cousin satin	origin aspirin	muffin raisin			**in**
Dissolve the aspirin in the basin, and then have your muffin.					
sign reign design feign assign	consign resign ensign countersign	condign benign align			**gn**
Sign a letter and a road sign.					
foreign	sovereign				**eign**
Fore**ign**: Why difficult? Fe**ign** from res**ign**ing.					

ng					Sound Group 38	
sing cling wing sting spring	flinging swinging stringing bringing					**ing**
song gong strong	belong furlong	songster thronging	billabong			**o ng**
Who belonged to the strong voice that sung the song by the billabong?						
boomerang slang fang hang sprang	gangway gangster hanger mustang	coat hanger				**a ng**
The Mustang sprang down the gangway when the gangster tried to hang on to her.						
rung flung swung hung lung	bungler stung					**u ng**
That stung when I was flung to the ground.						
length lengthy strength	lengthen lengthwise strengthen					**e ng**
Strengthen each length as you go.						
tongue harangue	tongue- tied meringue					**ngue**
The dog's sneaky tongue licked the meringue whilst no one was looking.						

finger angle mingle tingle bangle new- fangled	banker hunger monger	linger angry hungry bungler			n
The thinker put his finger through the bangle on an angle.					

d (at the end of the word)					Sound Group 39	
spade hide fade strode ride	explode stampede grenade provide	gratitude marmalade solitude coincide	barricade cavalcade insecticide escalade			de

Using his spade he hid the grenade until the cavalcade arrived.

| add
ladder
daddy
peddle
fiddle | bedding
ridden
coddle
nodding | paddle
budding | | | | dd |

Daddy please fiddle and fix my bedding.

| chopped
fined
stepped
hopped
filled
tried | finished
jumped
listed
missed
shocked | rubbed
inscribed
absorbed
advanced
managed | experienced
pronounced
experienced | | governed
rubbished | ed |

Adding "ed" to a verb creates the past tense.

| crowd
find
scald
word
herd
heard* | absurd
defend
record
orchard | remind
expand
resound
descend | found*
wound*
sold*
told* | | | d |

Every word he told the crowd was absurd.

| For words ending in **ld**, see Sound Group 11 **oul.** | | | | | | id |

💡 **These words, though the action is finished, do not end in ed. They may be easily formed from the present tense in the following manner:**

a. write the present tense: sell

b. say the past tense: sold

c. decide which sounds change...

d. change sell to sold

tell	told
find	found
hold	held
wind	wound
hear	heard
grind	ground

				b
baby bob bib bad bend bad	bamboo barber baboon bubble	barbaric barbecue Biblical		
Bobby the baby is really a baboon but hidden behind the bib it wore.				
bubbles scrabble squabble pebble nibble scribble	dabbling bobbing rubber rabbit cabbage	cobwebby rubbished snobbishly rubbery shabbily		**bb**
they squabbled over the bubbles.				
globe				**be**

pig pat pop pup pin poop	paper piping poplin puppy poppy	populate popular Papuan propeller propaganda	apart aperture aptitude apostrophe apology			p
Say quickly, "Pat the pig and Poppy the puppy pooped on the paper."						
puppy scrappy choppy snappy poppy happy	shopping shipping wrapping ripping dripping	pepper puppet trapper supper happen	appal appeal applaud appliance appreciative			pp
Puppy makes her happy when it eats her supper.						
grape						pe

h Sayings its sound (short sound)			**Sound Group 42**
hat			h
who? whom whole whose whoop	wholly wholesale wholesome whooping		wh

Index

A

B

C

H

Half-Long 15, 31
Historical or Etymological Diacritics 33

I

Implosives 24
Indefinite sound 53
Ingressive 24
In linguistic analysis 33
International Phonetic Association 13, 16

L

Labialised 14, 35
Labiodental 13, 25
Laminal 14, 35
Lateral Approximant 13
Lateral Fricative 13
Lateral Release 14, 36
Length Diacritics 32
Less Rounded 14, 35
Letter-based combinations 10
Letter combination iii, 52
Letter combinations iii, iv, vi, 1, 6, 7, 52
Letter-combinations iii, 4
Letter Combinations vi
Letter Sounds Combinations 3
Linguolabial 14, 34
Linking (Absence of a Break) 15, 31
Lips 11, 24, 25, 30, 35
Liquids 17, 44
Liquids 44
Long 15, 30, 31, 46
Lowered (= Voiced Bilabial Approximant) 14, 37

M

N

O

P

R

S